CW00641920

PRAISE FOR UNLOCK IT

"In a world where so many teach and very few actually lead, Dan has built an impressive following by helping others see the potential inside themselves and leading them by example to a place of true growth and change. The data doesn't lie—millions have watched, read, and listened to his videos, books, and podcasts. Entrepreneurs at any level can learn from his past and benefit not just from his selling strategies but also from his unique leadership strategies."

MATT MEAD | *Chairman, Grayson Pierce Capital* | *CEO, EpekData and BrandLync* | *@mattmead*

"Dan has been on a meteoric rise from one of Vancouver's most respected entrepreneurs to internationally recognized global educator. He has transformed the lives of thousands around the world, helping them make every moment count. The struggles, stories, and lessons that he writes about in *Unlock It* show Dan Lok is a man of principle and is creating a true impact on the world."

DWAYNE J. CLARK | *CEO, Áegis Living* | *@dwaynejclark*

"If you've loved any of Dan's previous works, *Unlock It* takes everything to the next level! Dan has the ability to educate, inspire, and motivate everyone from start-up entrepreneurs to successful seven- and eight-figure CEOs and business owners. He speaks words of wisdom few possess, due to his unique experiences, his growth through life, and his successful business empire. Whether you are a marketer, start-up, entrepreneur, millionaire, or current couch potato, *Unlock It* provides invaluable education, systems, and the ability to 'unlock' your true potential.

If you only plan to read one book this year, make this it."

RUDY MAWER | *Founder and CEO, ROI Machines* | *Two-Time Multi-Seven-Figure Business Owner and Facebook Ad Expert* | *@RudyMawerLife*

"In a world full of warm and fuzzy personalities evangelizing the narrative of everyone deserving a participation trophy in the battle for success, Dan Lok's new book *Unlock It* is the wake-up call so sorely needed. A true modern-day rags-to-riches success story, Dan lays bare what it truly takes to create success from any set of circumstances at a blistering pace.

Be warned, if you're seeking another politically correct book that allows you to hide comfortably from your potential, this book isn't for you, but if you're truly ready for a predictable, practical, and profitable path to success, you've now got the manual."

JONATHAN "JCRON" CRONSTEDT | *President, Kajabi.com*

"What I love about *Unlock It* is that Dan is able to speak to people at all stages of wealth and give practical, proven advice for every step of the way. I couldn't recommend this book more because it helps each of us let go of old mindsets, release current myths, and overcome essential wealth challenges—all of which can overwhelm anyone easily without these clear strategies and tactics. This is a great book for anyone who is looking for a proven way to move to their next wealth level—whatever it is!"

ANNE YATCH | *Cofounder, Plan Sight*

"Dan has taken his real-world experiences and condensed them into powerful, yet simple, lessons that allow people worldwide to achieve unparalleled success. Just say, 'I'm ready to learn,' and *unlock* the black belt training to *your* personal success!"

MICHAEL A. HALL | *Business Owner and Executive Advisor to CEOs, Culture Index*

"When you are a successful entrepreneur, one of the hardest tasks is deciding what to optimize when all is going well. *Unlock It* flipped a switch in my head. After reading it, I've become more focused on what to grow in my business using Dan's strategies. This book is for anyone who is hungry for more."

TORBEN PLATZER | *Founder and CEO, TPA Media* | *@torbenplatzer*

"Dan Lok is an impressive entrepreneur. Not only has he personally produced awesome results but he also genuinely wants others to take action and achieve exceptional results for themselves.

Dan teaches from his own experiences. He takes the lessons and principles he's learned along his journey and boils them down into simple strategies that can help you overcome new challenges on the path to achieving your next level of success."

BRIAN SCUDAMORE | *Founder & CEO, O2E Brands (1-800-GOT-JUNK?, WOW 1 DAY PAINTING, You Move Me, Shack Shine)* | *@BrianScudamore*

"I'm an author, entrepreneur, and Amazon consultant with a decade of experience. Dan's stories and spirit have inspired me to grow myself and further develop my high-income skills. Helping others expand their e-commerce businesses is my passion, and the strategies I've learned in *Unlock It* will help me to further 'unlock' my clients' and my success."

AKEMI SUE FISHER | *Founder and CEO, Love and Launch* | *@akemisue*

UNLOCK IT

DAN LOK

UNLOCK IT

THE MASTER KEY *to* WEALTH, SUCCESS, *and* SIGNIFICANCE

ForbesBooks

Published by ForbesBooks, Charleston, South Carolina.
Member of Advantage Media Group.

ForbesBooks is a registered trademark, and the ForbesBooks colophon is a trademark of Forbes Media, LLC.

Printed in the United States of America.

10 9 8 7 6 5 4 3 2 1

ISBN: 978-1-94663-375-0
LCCN: 2019912759

Cover design by Carly Blake.
Interior design by Lara Frayre and Carly Blake.

Advantage Media Group is proud to be a part of the Tree Neutral® program. Tree Neutral offsets the number of trees consumed in the production and printing of this book by taking proactive steps such as planting trees in direct proportion to the number of trees used to print books. To learn more about Tree Neutral, please visit **www.treeneutral.com**.

Since 1917, the Forbes mission has remained constant. Global Champions of Entrepreneurial Capitalism. ForbesBooks exists to further that aim by bringing the Stories, Passion, and Knowledge of top thought leaders to the forefront. ForbesBooks brings you The Best in Business. To be considered for publication, please visit **www.forbesbooks.com**.

To my wife, Jennie Li, for being my best friend and partner.
You're more than I could ask for.
Behind every successful man, there's a smarter woman.
Thank you for being the smarter woman in my life.

To my mom, who loves and supports me no matter what.

To my dad, who I wish could see this book.

To my team, who dedicate their lives to helping our organization realize our vision and execute our mission.

To Peter Lu, who worked countless late nights editing this book.

To Charlie Fusco, who pushed me to write this book.

To my students and mentees from all over the world.
It's an honor to teach you.

To you, for striving to be a better version of yourself.

CONTENTS

Introduction

I don't know why you're reading this book.

Maybe you're waiting in the airport, and the book cover caught your attention. You're flipping through this book wondering whether you should pick it up or not. Or maybe a friend of yours gave you this book. Possibly, you're one of my fans on social media and familiar with who I am.

No. I don't know why you're reading this book. One thing I do know is that if you're reading this book, you want more.

You see, many people are not interested in improving their life in any shape or form. Very often, they feel stuck, as if they don't have the power to change and accept life as is.

But YOU are different.

You believe in something else. You believe you have the desire to change, the ability to succeed, and that you can be a better version of you.

You believe you have the power to unlock your destiny.

Now, you might have read a lot of different books on success, self-improvement, wealth, and business already. This book may not be your first "personal development rodeo." Even though you learn a lot from different books and they teach you many different things, let me ask you a question.

Do you feel deep down there's still a missing piece? Like you're putting together a jigsaw puzzle, and you have some pieces, but you never get to see the whole picture?

You're looking for that missing link. You're looking for that piece of information that connects all the dots. You're looking for that key that unlocks everything else for you.

You're looking for that missing link. You're looking for that piece of information that connects all the dots. You're looking for that key that unlocks everything else for you.

If that's you, then my goal is to give you that key.

I hope that this book will not only give you a new perspective, but more importantly, a road map to implement everything you've learned in the past and to connect those learnings in a clear, concise manner.

Chances are, if you've read other books, what I'm sharing with you is nothing you haven't heard of before.

I don't claim to be a super original thinker. The truth is, I think originality is highly overrated. You can always tell who the pioneer is when they are lying on the ground with arrows in their back.

No, I'm not an original thinker. I'm an entrepreneur. I'm a synthesizer. I take ideas, make them better, and execute them better than most.

Absorb what is useful, discard what is not, add what is uniquely your own.

BRUCE LEE

Most books will tell you to do this and don't do that; don't do this and do that instead. That's not what I'm here to do. This book is here to share with you a new perspective and a system that shows you how to think differently.

My challenge as an educator is to change the way you think. Changing the way you think will alter the way you do things. The exciting part for me is that inevitably the way you do things will force you to produce different results.

Now, there will be information that I share that you may or may not agree with. That's perfectly fine. Everything I teach comes from my experience, so it doesn't make it right. It doesn't make it wrong either; it just makes it my experience.

All I can do is come from my own experience.

I ask that you read this book cafeteria-style. Take what seems useful and implement it. If it works, great—keep it. If it doesn't work, that's okay too—throw it away. No hard feelings. That's how I believe we all should learn.

WHY AM I WRITING THIS BOOK AFTER TEN YEARS OF SILENCE?

In my twenties I published about a dozen books, including a best-selling book that sold over one hundred thousand copies worldwide. I thought that was my last book, and I haven't thought about writing another book for ten years.

So why am I writing this book? Why now?

People have been asking for this book.

Over the last decade, my mission has been to start a global economic movement by empowering people and developing their High-Income Skills. As I met with my students and fans around the world, I listened to their stories.

I've heard countless stories of college students coming out of school, and they can't get a job. Even though they've studied in school for four years, their employers will tell them in interviews that they don't have enough experience.

So they go back to school and get further into debt; they get an MBA or a second degree and work even harder. Now when they sit across the table from the employer, they say they have too much experience. Sometimes, the jobs they prepare to get will become extinct by the time they get out of school.

So what do you do? They feel handcuffed even though they did what they were supposed to do. It's not just students who are struggling. Entrepreneurs come up to me and share their pain.

They have trouble getting their products noticed, they can't get anything to sell, their operating costs are going up, and costs are rising, and there's more on the line. Technology is lowering the barrier to entry and making the marketplace more competitive than ever.

Overall, it's just getting more challenging to run a business. Even successful entrepreneurs who have "made it" come up to me and share with me their concerns about staying in business.

They're not sure if the success they've built is going to last or how to sustain their success or how to take it to the next level. New technologies are going to come and wipe out their entire business.

They know social media is powerful, and they know a new way of doing business is emerging, but they're not sure how to adapt to this change. Now that they've achieved a taste of financial success, they understand that the name of the game is not getting rich; the name of the game is staying rich.

WHAT YOU'LL GET FROM THIS BOOK

In my past twenty years of business and life, I've picked up key lessons and principles that have helped turn me from a poor Asian immigrant with $150,000 in debt to a leader of a global organization. When I've followed these lessons, I've succeeded. When I've disobeyed these principles, I've failed. So whether you want to excel in your career, carve out a path on your own, or build a company that lasts, you'll find useful ideas here.

First, you'll get to know me very well. You'll see how I wasn't given anything in life and how I was able to rise from nothing to something.

From my journey, one key concept that has guided my philosophy about financial success is the Wealth Triangle. In chapter 1, I'll introduce you to the Wealth Triangle and why (contrary to popular belief) starting a business is a horrible first step to achieving wealth and success. There are three steps to the Wealth Triangle—and most people do things in the wrong order. I'll show you the right sequence to achieve the milestones in the Wealth Triangle.

I'll introduce you to the six universal Wealth Archetypes. These are archetypes and profiles that will help you identify your relationship with money and where you are on your wealth journey. After you get clarity on where you are, you'll be able to start the first step of the Wealth Triangle.

The first step of the Wealth Triangle is attaining the High-Income Skill that will help you pay the bills. It's a skill that will help you become recession proof. Most successful CEOs and entrepreneurs didn't start with a business as their first step; they began with a High-Income Skill. In chapter 3, you'll learn about the power of a High-Income Skill and why debt problems are skill problems in disguise.

Even with a High-Income Skill, there is a metaskill most people don't have. That skill is the art of achieving maximum productivity. In chapter 5, you'll learn how to achieve maximum results in minimum time. This chapter won't be a chapter on time management—far from it. You'll see why productivity is self-mastery, and you'll see how a few simple adjustments to your current routine could multiply your results.

After achieving maximum personal productivity, you'll learn how to achieve maximum financial productivity. Whether you want to move up in your company, become your own boss, or empower your employees with a powerful skill, this chapter will show you a new brand of sales. You'll learn about High-Ticket Closing® and how you can close deals and negotiations more effectively without using any slimy, sleazy, or high-pressure tactics.

In chapter 7, we'll be looking at the second step of the Wealth Triangle—the Scalable Business. You'll learn about the three pillars of business growth and how to grow your revenues at an exponential rate. Most businesses have one or two pillars working for them, but without all three pillars working in tandem, they are leaving opportunity on the table.

One of the most critical factors in determining the longevity of a business is its profit margin. In chapter 8, you'll learn how to increase your profit margin by selling at higher prices. You'll see how it gives you a competitive edge when it comes to advertising, testing and research, and scaling your business.

Lastly, you'll get a look inside into what I think is one of the most overlooked assets to any business. It's what I call Social Capital. In today's age, I believe social capital is even more important than financial capital. It's the secret behind why a twenty-one-year-old Kylie Jenner was able to become the youngest billionaire in history. If you have a company or a brand you want to grow and sustain, this chapter will give you a framework for expanding your own social capital.

If you're ready to begin, then flip the page.

CHAPTER 0

How I Unlocked My Success, Wealth, and Significance

THE POOR ASIAN IMMIGRANT BOY

This entire story starts with an affair.

I was born in Hong Kong. I loved both my parents, but they did not love each other. When I was still in the womb, my dad had an affair. Though my mom was hurt and angry, she didn't want her son to grow up in a broken family. So she stayed. But when I was fourteen years old, my mom couldn't take it anymore and decided to bring me with her to another country—Canada. We became immigrants in a new and unfamiliar country with no connections, no money, and not a single word of English on our lips.

My mom, who was a housewife, suddenly had to become the provider. I had to adapt to a completely different environment. The first few days were full of fear and anxiety. We lived in Surrey—one of the most dangerous neighborhoods in Vancouver. It took me three days before I could gather the courage to step outside our tiny one-bedroom apartment and walk down the street.

I was one of only three Chinese kids in the entire school, and if you think racism didn't exist in Canada, my experience tells a different story. At school, I was the invisible kid. I couldn't speak a word of English and couldn't make any friends. I would sit in the back of the room, and I never put my hand up. After school, I'd go straight to my locker and grab my backpack without looking at or making eye contact with anyone in the hallway. I was too shy to even walk in the middle of the hall, so I'd walk along the sides. I was that kid you could go to school with for semesters, and you wouldn't even know his name. If you look at my group graduation photo, you'll see all the popular kids together, and I was alone in the corner with no one around me.

So the bullies targeted me.

At lunchtime, these three big guys would drag me from the front door of the school to the grass field, and they'd beat the hell out of me. Maybe they thought I was an easy target. I only weighed 105 pounds—I looked like a twig. They threw me to the ground, ganged up around me, and just kicked and punched me as I was down. The beatings happened multiple times. Today, you can still see a scar on my chin.

Once during this time, my mom bought me as a birthday gift an electronic dictionary that could translate English words into Chinese. It was $300—that we could not afford—but my mom saved up for and bought it because she wanted the best for me. I treasured it. I brought it with me to school every day, and I plugged in words I couldn't understand so that I could follow along in class. I worked hard at it every single day. I was finally making an advancement. Maybe I could eventually raise my hand in class or make some new friends.

One day, the same three kids saw me using the electronic dictionary. They came up to me and said, "Hey, why are you doing math during lunch? You nerd. Give me that." At first, I didn't understand the situation. I tried explaining to them, "No, this is a dictionary. My mom bought it for me. Please give it back." But they didn't listen. They passed it around to each other, threw it over my head when I was trying to get it back, and then ...

CRACK!

They threw it out the window. We were on the second floor. I heard the impact on the pavement below, and I knew $300 of my mom's hard-earned money was down the drain. I was pissed.

But more importantly, I didn't want my mom to find out. I didn't want her to find out that her hard work was for nothing. I didn't want her to be hurt again. So at home I went through the motions with the broken electronic dictionary, pretending it was working, but at school, I got a paper dictionary from the library. I looked up every word I was supposed to be learning and read it out loud at least fifty times to make sure I could say it correctly.

Have you ever felt like the world was just against you even though you did nothing wrong? That's how I felt. These are just a few examples of many, many incidents.

THE AFTERNOON THAT TURNED MY WORLD UPSIDE DOWN

One afternoon, I dropped off my school bag on the sleeping bag that I slept on in the living room, and I noticed that my mom's door was closed, and she was speaking on the phone with someone. When the call ended, she came out of her room. I'll never forget her face. She had tears streaming down her cheeks. It looked like she had been crying the entire day. She looked hopeless.

"Mom, what's wrong?"

"Your dad called. He can't send us money anymore."

"What? What do you mean?"

"His business ... his business went bankrupt."

I believe every person has a moment in their lives when everything changes for them. It changes them at their core, and they can never go back to being the same again. These are what I call "defining moments." Most people think inspirational or happy moments shape them. It's not true. Happiness doesn't change you; pain does.

> ***Defining moments hurt like hell; they break you. They tear you into little pieces and test your resolve. If you make it through, you become a better version of yourself—a renewed version.***

Defining moments hurt like hell; they break you. They tear you into little pieces and test your resolve. If you make it through, you become a better version of you—a renewed version. Defining moments are deceptive because you don't feel your life changing as they happen. These moments can feel more like a painful slam against the concrete as you hit rock bottom; you go into shock as your whole world starts falling around you. Moments that change your life feel like you can't get enough air in your lungs; I know because it is exactly how I felt when my mom came out of her room. That's what it felt like when I, Dan Lok, had to step up and become a man.

Everything I have ever done wasn't for the money. I just never wanted to see my mom cry again. At that moment, I promised that no matter what it took, I never wanted to see that look on my mom's face again. That's what started my entrepreneurial journey.

THE FIRST $100 IS THE SWEETEST

At first, I thought getting a job would be the solution to all my money problems. "If you want to earn money, then get a job!" That's what everyone said, so I listened to them and got a job bagging groceries at a Chinese supermarket.

I made minimum wage working ten-hour shifts and stood on my feet doing the same mind-numbing repetitive motions over and over again. I had very little patience for a job like that, and I quit after a few months.

"There has to be a better way to earn money. But how?" I thought to myself. That's when my first idea hit me.

One day I was jogging in my neighborhood, and I saw an older gentleman, probably in his seventies, who was mowing his lawn very slowly. It looked like he was having trouble, so I asked him if he needed any help with mowing his lawn. He agreed, and I finished the job for him. As I was leaving, he stopped me and pulled out $20.

That's when the light bulb came on. I could do this for other people and make more money! That was the start of my first business—a lawn-mowing business. I was just a kid and couldn't afford a lawn mower, but I was smart enough to make a deal with the older gentleman.

"Hey, it seems like the lawn mower is a bit too heavy for you to use. How about I mow your lawn every week for FREE, and you let me use it for my business?"

He thought about it for a moment. "Ah, sure, why not. I don't use it that much anyways."

BOOM. I had just closed my first deal.

However, having a service to offer was only the first step. The next step was selling the service. So I knocked on every door in my neighborhood to ask if my neighbors needed their lawns mowed—and I got rejected at every single house. I felt awful, AND I still had to mow the older gentleman's lawn—for free. Then my next "brilliant" idea came. My aunt had a printing business. She printed out flyers, but she needed someone to distribute them for her.

"Auntie, I'll hand out your flyers for FREE—if you let me advertise my lawn-mowing business on the backside of the flyers!"

She thought about it for a moment. Then she replied, "Why not? I need someone to help me hand these out anyway."

BOOM. Another business deal closed.

When my aunt agreed to let me hand out her flyers with my business on the back, I thought I would be making thousands of dollars that week. I made grand plans for what I would do with the money. I was even worried about how I would balance school with my booming business success. With this newfound inspiration and determination, I handed out five thousand flyers. Then I went home and sat next to my phone, waiting for the calls to come rolling in.

One hour went by ... no calls. One day went by ... no calls. Three days went by ... no calls. Did I put the wrong number on the back? No. I checked; it was the right number. So why wasn't anyone calling? They had lawns that needed mowing, so why wasn't anyone calling me?

By the end of my first "marketing campaign," I made a big fat zero.

I thought back to my first "client," the older gentleman. What did I do differently? That's when it hit me—the first lesson I learned that still affects how I do business today. I mowed the older gentleman's lawn FIRST and THEN got the sale.

Armed with this epiphany, I went to a higher-end neighborhood in the area and saw a house with grass that went up to my waist. That was my opportunity. I brought my lawn mower, I mowed the lawn, and I sat on the front porch waiting for the owner to come home.

When the owner came home, she didn't even recognize her place. She drove past and had to reverse back because her lawn was so much shorter.

"What's going on here?" she asked.

"Well, ma'am ... I'm just a kid trying to make some money, and I saw your lawn was growing out so much that I thought I'd help out."

To my surprise, she was really grateful.

"Oh, thank you! My husband is always working, so he doesn't have time for taking care of the lawn. Here's $100 for your trouble."

BOOM. I got my first $100 deal, and the first $100 is always the sweetest.

A word of warning: What I did was utterly ILLEGAL. You can't just go onto someone's property and start mowing the lawn. I do NOT recommend doing what I did. I was just a dumb kid trying to make some money.

You have to start somewhere, right?

HOW TO GET $150,000 IN DEBT IN THREE YEARS—GUARANTEED

After starting my lawn-mowing business at seventeen and realizing it wasn't going to make me rich in the long term, I started jumping into other entrepreneurial ideas.

Maybe you can relate to this. When I was "evaluating" business ideas, I thought every opportunity I found was going to be the "next big thing." Over the next three years, I tried everything. From vending machines to fixing computers to delivery services to network marketing—if it had a remote chance of making money, I'd jump in, which was very. VERY. Dumb. I failed at thirteen different businesses before I had my first success, but nothing hurt more than the last business.

I was already $120,000 in debt from losing my first twelve businesses. I had maxed out my credit cards, borrowed money from all my aunts and uncles, and even borrowed some money from my mom. I was relentless. I still believed that I could make it all work. At the time, I was still with the network marketing company. I had already burned bridges with most of my friends and family because all I could ever talk about was the company and how great it was. Have you ever had a friend ask you to go out for coffee to offer you a shady "business opportunity"? That was me. My friends and family started avoiding me because all I could talk about was getting them involved in my network marketing opportunity.

Without friends or family to target, I had to find other ways to recruit people onto my team. So I had another "genius idea" and started placing my business card in office buildings, hoping someone would reach out and have coffee with me.

To my surprise, one person called me. We met up for coffee, and I went through my presentation with him. I told him how great my company was and how easy it would be to make money.

"You need to find three people to join your team. Then they get another three people to join their team. So before you know it, you'll get to retire."

"Dan, I'm gonna stop you right there."

"Huh? I was getting to the best part."

"No, your presentation was great. But I've got something better for you. You seem like a sharp guy, and I was looking for someone just like you to help me out in my business."

He went on to explain how he built websites and sold them to people for massive profits. If I could help him fund the start-up phase of his business, we'd split the profits as partners.

Remember when I said if an opportunity sounded like it had even a remote chance of making money, I'd jump into it? Well, I'm a man of my word.

I went into that business with him as "partners." I invested $1,000 at first, then $2,000, and then $5,000. Every time we'd meet in his office, he'd tell me that we're close to breaking through, that we need a bit more time and money to finish the developments. Like the naive young kid I was, I believed him. I kept putting money into it: $10,000 ... $15,000 ... $20,000 ... then $25,000. I was deep into this business. I was determined to make it work.

Now at this point, you might be asking, "Dan, where are you getting all this money?" Great question. It was from the last remaining person who believed in me—my mom.

I had already maxed out my credit cards and borrowed money from every relative that would lend me money. So when my new "business partner" showed up, I could only turn to my mom.

I remember the day my "business partner" asked me for one final investment of $5,000. He told me this was the last one, and that was all we needed to strike it rich. Of course, I believed him.

ONE OF THE MOST SHAMEFUL MOMENTS OF MY LIFE

I drove my mom to the bank so that we could withdraw the last $5,000 that I needed. My mom was already near her account limit. While we were in the line, she was grabbing my arm and crying, "Don't do this, Dan. Don't do this."

Like a crazed gambler, I told her, "Mom, just believe in me. I know I can make this work." She was still crying and clutching my arm when we withdrew the final $5,000.

Later that day, I brought the $5,000 to the man and asked him if that was all he needed. He said yes and that everything would be finished soon. Then I went home with the hope that this was my big break. One day went by—no message from him. Two days went by—no message. Three days—no sign from him. I called his cell phone—no response. I called his office—it said the number did not exist. What the hell was going on here?

I rushed to his office, and everything was gone. I called every number I could think of that was associated with him—the secretary, the offices next to his. I even asked the janitor. No one knew anything about this man. They were as clueless as I was. He disappeared without a trace. I was scammed. At that moment, I was so full of anger, hatred, and shame. I was furious at myself.

"How could I have let this happen? Why am I so stupid? How could I have lost all my mom's money? Why do I keep making dumb mistakes like this?"

As I was walking home, trying to think of what I would tell my mom, I came across a bridge. I looked over. It was high enough to kill someone if they jumped off.

"Maybe I should end it here. Maybe my mom is better off if I didn't keep losing all her money."

I continued to stand there.

"Maybe she would be better off if I didn't exist."

Luckily, I'm still alive today. There was a small part of me that knew I couldn't leave my mom alone in this world. I knew that I had to man up and take care of my mom.

"THIS SUCKS. DO IT AGAIN."

After picking myself up, I started attending more seminars and workshops to sharpen my skills. At one of the seminars, I met my first mentor, Alan Jacques.

Now if you don't know Alan, he's the founder of Real Estate Investor Network (REIN), the largest real estate network at that time. He was the first person to bring Robert Kiyosaki—author of *Rich Dad Poor Dad*—to Canada, before Robert was famous. For about a year, I worked for Alan for next to nothing. Every day for the first few months, I licked hundreds of envelopes for mailings. Then I moved on to helping Alan edit some of his sales letters. After a while, Alan let me write my first sales letter (a letter we sent out to people to let them know about our products and services). I spent days and nights crafting a sales letter, making sure every sentence and word was correct. When I gave it to Alan, he told me, "This sucks. Do it again."

I brought it back to him, and again, he told me, "This sucks. Do it again." I did it AGAIN and made sure it was the best thing I ever wrote. I gave it to him, and he looked at it for a second longer this time, "It's still no good. Once more." We went back at it about six or seven times before Alan finally said it was good enough to send out.

The funny thing is, years later Alan told me, "You know, Dan, the first letter you wrote was pretty good. But I needed to challenge you. You thought you'd given it your best, but that was not your best. The second time, you thought it was your best. There was a gap between what you thought was your best compared to your actual best. Being able to see this difference and make the necessary changes is how you get better at this skill."

THE ONE-MAN "MAD MEN" AGENCY

After I learned to be a copywriter from Alan, I branched out and started my one-person advertising agency. At first, I was selling my services for $500 to $1,000, but because I had only so many hours of work I could do in a day, the number of clients I could take on was limited. I knew I had to charge more if I wanted to support me and my mom. I had only done copywriting for a few months, so I didn't think I could charge more than $1,000. That's when Alan challenged me again.

"Dan, you should bump up your price. One thousand dollars is too low."

"I guess so. What're you thinking, bump it up 10 percent? To $1,100? That's pretty reasonable."

"No. Double it."

"What do you mean? I can't double it. I've only been doing it for a few months! I'm a twenty-one-year-old kid with a thick accent; I can't double my price!"

"Dan. Double it."

I sighed. "Okay."

Alan told me to practice asking for the price in front of the mirror. I listened and went in front of the mirror,

"How much do you charge?" I asked myself in the mirror.

"T-t-t-two thousand dollars." I stuttered.

"How much do you charge?"

"T-two thousand dollars."

"How much do you charge?"

"Two thousand dollars."

I kept practicing until I could say the price with a straight face and without stuttering. Guess what? When the next prospect asked me how much I charged, I told him $2,000 and there was no pushback. A few months later, I had a couple of $2,000 clients and was feeling pretty good. Until Alan came to me and said,

"Dan, it's time. Double it."

"What? Double it again? I'm going to lose all my clients!"

"Double it."

"No way they're going to pay that much for me. How am I going to pay the bills if I lose all my clients?"

"Dan. Double it."

"Okay."

I repeated the process and followed Alan's instructions. To my surprise, it worked again. There was no pushback. I repeated the process a few months later, raising the amount to $8,000. Then $10,000. Within the span of a year, I went from charging $1,000 to $10,000 for doing the same amount of work. That's when I learned you don't always have to work harder to earn more money; sometimes it's just about communicating your value better than your competitors. From that lesson,

I was able to achieve Security. I was ready to provide for my mom, get a new car, and pay off all of my debt.

MORE SUCCESS THAN I COULD IMAGINE

After I achieved Security through copywriting, I found great success by starting multiple online businesses. I had a copywriting background, so I was one of the first to enter the online market. I had a massive advantage over everyone else. With my copywriting expertise paired with the internet, money started coming in faster than I could ever imagine as a kid. One day, when I was twenty-seven years old, I looked at my bank account and realized I had $1 million. This money was the "success" I was chasing this entire time. I had "made it." From being an immigrant boy making minimum wage at a supermarket, I somehow had become a young millionaire. After so many years of working hard, it was finally time to relax, so I went to the beach.

For the next month, I didn't do any work. I went to English Bay, the beach in downtown Vancouver, and sipped cold drinks while looking at the ocean—what most people would imagine as a dream retirement. It was enjoyable at first, but then I did it again the next day. And then the next day. And then the next day. And believe it or not, sitting on a blanket of sand doing nothing for an entire week is pretty boring (and you get sunburned too). So the following month, I watched six or seven movies every day. When you watch that many movies, guess what? You don't like movies so much anymore!

I was in a position most people dream of getting to in life. They had to wait until sixty-five to do what I was doing at twenty-seven, but I was bored and miserable. Everything that would supposedly make me happy didn't make me happy. I had everything I ever wanted and more, and yet I still felt unfulfilled.

I DON'T KNOW WHY I'M CRYING

One day I woke up with tears coming down my cheek. My wife, Jennie, saw this and was concerned. She asked, "Why are you crying? What's wrong?"

"I don't know. Tears are just coming down my cheek."

"Are you feeling okay? Are you in pain? Do you need to go to the hospital?"

"No, I don't know why. I just have this feeling of depression coming over me. I don't know where it's coming from."

I felt empty inside. I had worked hard to get to where I was. I lived a good life. I had all of the money I could wish for in my life. All my needs were taken care of and then some. I had the freedom to do what I wanted to do. But I was still miserable for no apparent reason. I questioned everything: "What am I chasing exactly? Why did I work so hard? What was I working for?" And as cliché as it sounds, I wondered, "Is there more to life than just this?"

From that point on, I went on a spiritual journey. I dove deep into personal development and spiritual work. I thought it was all about money and results, and that the spiritual "woo-woo" stuff was fluff. But after my experience, I realized there was some truth to these teachings. As silly as it sounds for a young multimillionaire, I wanted to find myself. I spent all my life chasing achievements, believing they would lead me to happiness. However, I discovered that what I craved was not an achievement but fulfillment. I mistakenly thought money would give me meaning. I was trying to win the race of accomplishment by running on the track of success. I asked myself a simple question that might be useful for you as well:

"When am I the happiest?"

The answer became clear. When I was in college, I had a couple of martial arts students I taught free of charge. I loved it. When I was teaching, I got into a flow, and time disappeared. I loved watching people light up and transform right in front of my eyes. Teaching gave me a thrill. I loved teaching.

Many people these days say, "I love this so much I'll do it for free." I can't entirely agree with that. I believe you should love what you do so much that you say to yourself, "I love this so much; it's the only thing I'll do for money." To this day, I'm the happiest when I am teaching. However, at the time, I had only taught martial arts and had never thought of making a living as a martial arts teacher. I asked myself, "How can I teach more? How can I build a business that combines my purpose, profit, and passion? How can I make it so that it's ALL I do?" That's when I became a full-time teacher. That's when I started living a life that was fully aligned and fully congruent with my beliefs. That was when I moved into the final stage of my life: Significance.

TO LIVE A LIFE YOU WILL LOVE, ASK YOURSELF THIS ONE QUESTION

"Would you still do what you do if you won the lottery?" For most people, the answer is, "No, I'd quit immediately. I'd stop what I'm doing right now." I can say without hesitation that I would be doing precisely the same thing as what I'm doing right now. How can I be so confident? Well, I have made way more money than a lottery jackpot, and I'm still doing the same thing today. I'm very grateful every day of my life.

I'm able to utilize my skills, expertise, and experience to impact millions of people's lives. I live a stress-free lifestyle and get to do what I love. There are people with world-class talent who buy into our vision, mission, and culture, and I get to spend time with and learn from amazing people every day.

IMPACTING MILLIONS AROUND THE WORLD

I get mail from my students almost every day. It could be a simple postcard, a package of their hometown food, or even a portrait of me made from gemstones.

I'm not trying to impress you or show that I'm so great. It's just an indication of the appreciation that my students have for our community. In our society, we see success stories from our students every day—stories of them quitting their jobs, paying off their mortgage, and buying their parents' well-deserved trips. Not only that, you can see how my students carry themselves with a newfound sense of dignity and confidence.

I also get to meet my students at our annual private event in Vancouver. Thousands of my students fly in from all over the world to share a fantastic weekend. I get to hear all their heartwarming stories in person. I love and treasure every single one.

I've been lucky enough to grow a following of millions on global media platforms like YouTube, Facebook, and Instagram that allow me to speak with people from places like Canada, the United States, Hong Kong, Singapore, Vietnam, Thailand, India, Germany, France, England, Scotland, Nigeria, Egypt, and many, many more. When you focus on making a meaningful impact on others, money comes faster, more naturally, and with less effort. I just wanted to teach and help as many people as I could. I never imagined that I'd be able to make such a great living at the same time.

DOING WHAT YOU LOVE TO DO

The majority of my days are spent doing the things I love to do:

- Reading books and learning
- Teaching and mentoring students
- Traveling with my wife and friends
- Strategizing, thinking, and planning for the future
- Practicing Jeet Kune Do—my favorite martial art
- Meeting and learning from world-class entrepreneurs and founders

Other than that, I don't do much "work." For me, I define work as anything I don't want to do. I have a team that takes care of those things for me so I can focus on what inspires me the most and leaves the most significant impact. Rarely do I need to worry about what's happening day to day in the business. If there is a fire that needs to be put out, my team will let me know. More often, they will solve the problem themselves.

Right now I work four and a half days a week: Monday to Thursday and a half day on Friday. I could work less, more, or not at all if I wanted to, but this setup is what makes me happiest right now. Occasionally, I'll take a week or two off to visit my mom in Asia or have a spontaneous trip with my wife. Other times, I'll fly to different cities to meet with other members of the Young Presidents' Organization (YPO) to see what ideas I can bring back to my team. If you're not familiar with YPO, it's an elite group of entrepreneurs and CEOs from around the world. According to its website, members are responsible for $9 trillion in annual revenue in the United States and employ twenty-two million people globally. If you hang around these heavy hitters, you'll start getting great ideas whether you like it or not.

So, if you were to ask me, "What do you do on a day-to-day basis?" my answer would be, "Whatever I want."

THE FOUR STAGES OF LIFE

At this stage of my life, I've gone through a lot. I've had my share of successes and failures. I've made money and lost money, met many great people and a lot of bad people, and I've had plenty of ups and downs. From my experiences and observations, I believe there are four stages of life we all go through as we strive for more in life: Survival, Security, Success, and Significance.

They happen in order, and there's no guarantee that everyone will make it to Significance. As you'll see, each stage requires more of you than the previous step. Let's talk about the first stage.

STAGE ONE: SURVIVAL

The main concern is taking care of you and paying the bills. You might be in debt, broke, or living paycheck to paycheck—whatever it is, your main focus is surviving. You feel like you are drowning and are gasping for air.

I was stuck here for the longest time. However, if you push through and begin taking more responsibility for your life, you'll make it to Security.

STAGE TWO: SECURITY

When you achieve Security, you have some breathing room. You have a place to live, a car to drive, and food to eat. You're no longer worried about the payments that are due next week. This stage is where most people stay.

They can pay the bills, but they get complacent. They have a decent life, a modest house, a decent car, and a respectable job. They don't play to win. They play to lose because they're afraid of taking any risk and losing what they already have. It took me years to reach this Security, but I'm glad I didn't stop at this stage. I continued to strive for Success because I thought that's what would bring me happiness.

STAGE THREE: SUCCESS

Now you have everything you need AND everything you want for yourself. You're driving nice cars, living in your dream home, and doing whatever you want, whenever you want. Many people look up to you because you're a leader of your industry—you're living the life.

However, when you stay here for too long, you realize there's a void—something is missing. You won't be able to pinpoint what is lacking in life. Most people think that to fill the emptiness, they need to achieve more. I spent ten years of my life chasing success, and when I reached this stage, I felt that same void. I tried to fill the void with more achievements, but I didn't find true fulfillment until I moved into the last stage: Significance.

STAGE FOUR: SIGNIFICANCE

You have everything you need AND want, but now you realize true fulfillment comes from helping and developing others. You recognize that success is getting what you want, while Significance is giving what you have. When you are living in this stage, you wake up with gratitude, abundance, and a sense of joy inside you.

You strive for more, yet you're content with what you have. You have ambitious goals, yet you are not attached. You are strong, yet you are not rigid. You have nothing to prove, yet you are achieving more than ever before. You plan for the future, yet you're fully present. You are in full flow with life—not against it. Since I decided to help and impact more people, many people have told me I've changed—I'm more easygoing and relaxed, yet they see me achieving more than I ever have. They ask me, "Dan, how do you do it?"

It's because I stopped focusing on success and moved toward Significance.

UNLOCK IT EXERCISE

- Which financial stage are you in right now?

  ____

- At which financial stage do you want to be?

  ____

WHAT'S NEXT?

You've heard my story, and now it's time to unlock your own.

Now that you understand the financial stages, the next chapter will show you how to move to the financial stage you want.

CHAPTER 1

Unlock Your Wealth

The world is full of inequality: racial inequality, gender inequality, education inequality, political inequality, and, of course, economic inequality. You can see that the rich are getting richer, and the poor are getting poorer—the middle class is disappearing. Now, is this fair? I don't know. All I know is that it's what's happening right now.

On top of the economic inequality, students are coming out of college unprepared and at a disadvantage. The September 2018 issue of *U.S. News & World Report* reported that the average fees at private national universities increased 168 percent, out-of-state tuition rose 200 percent at public national universities, and in-state fees (that are supposed to be the most affordable) at public national universities grew by 243 percent in just the last twenty years. College tuition is rising, and income levels are not keeping pace. While many baby boomers can remember working through college and graduating with little to no debt, this is not possible for most college students today.

With all the instability and uncertainty surrounding the future, people are looking for answers more than ever. While it is true that information is more accessible than ever, it's also true that misinformation is more accessible than ever.

So in this chapter, I'm going to dispel some of the most dangerous "Wealth Myths" that I believe hold people back financially. At the end of the chapter, you'll also see my Wealth Triangle concept that will give insight into how you can advance in your financial life.

Let's get started.

THE FOUR MOST DANGEROUS WEALTH MYTHS

WEALTH MYTH #1: HUSTLE AND WORK HARDER

Hustle. Work your face off. Work until you drop. Work until you're exhausted and then work some more.

If working hard is the secret to success, then why aren't garbage collectors millionaires? There are millions of hardworking construction workers, janitors, waiters, and cooks who do not earn enough money to live comfortably. If the secret to success is working hard, then a lot more people would be wealthier and happier.

At my first job, I bagged groceries at a supermarket and made $10 an hour. I stood for hours on end. My back would hurt, my feet would hurt, and I dreaded going to work every day. Fast-forward some years later, and now I charge $10,000 an hour for my consultation fees. My hourly rate went from $10 to $10,000—what changed? Well, I'm pretty much the same guy. I didn't have a degree then, and I still don't have a degree now. I still speak with a thick accent. I'm still the same Dan Lok; the only difference is the value I can deliver to the marketplace. Money is nothing more than the by-product of value creation.

Lok-It-In

MONEY IS NOTHING MORE THAN THE BY-PRODUCT OF VALUE CREATION.

If you ask most people how to make more money, they will tell you to work harder—"Get a second job, get another shift, put in overtime." I call this the "shotgun approach." You spray and pray. You try everything, spread your energy across different tasks, and hope that one of them will give you the results you want. The results, like the approach, are diluted.

But instead of working more hours, what if you increase the value of your hours? What if you learned to solve bigger problems for other people? What if you improved your skills and delivered more value?

Bagging groceries is a very easy problem to solve—almost anyone can do it. However, being a company consultant and helping in the development of successful marketing campaigns—that's a much more difficult problem to solve. When you look at it this way, you can see how money is tied more to the value you deliver—NOT the amount of work you put in. Focus on improving your skills and increasing the value you can give. Your income will follow these changes.

WEALTH MYTH #2: START A BUSINESS

Have you ever seen pictures on Instagram, Facebook, and YouTube showing the lifestyle of a "successful entrepreneur"? You know what I mean. The photos are showing off the cars they drive, their vacation spots, the homes they live in, and the life that they lead. It's easy to look at that and think to ourselves: "I want that life too, so I'm going to start a business just like them. Then I'm going to drive a fancy car, live in a fancy house, have a model girlfriend, and travel to all the best places in the world."

Well, sorry to break it to you. Most people AREN'T ready to start a business. Why? Because most people start businesses for the wrong reasons. When someone tells me they want to start a business, I ask them why. Usually, I hear one of three things:

1. I want more MONEY.
2. I want more FREEDOM.
3. I want more TIME.

The problem is that most entrepreneurs are NOT entrepreneurs. They are employees suffering from an entrepreneurial seizure. What does this mean? Most people who want to start a business are employees who either hate their jobs and want to escape, or they think they can do a better job running a business than their boss. They think, "I'm going to fire my boss, do my own thing, and be my own boss," but they go into a business with an employee mind-set.

A warning: owning a business will NOT give you more free time. It's like caring for a baby. Babies and businesses need to be nurtured and fed; they require constant attention and care. New business owners have less, not more, free time. In the beginning, you'll usually be wearing many hats, doing everything from bookkeeping to closing deals to delivery to marketing to customer service and on and on.

If you're already an entrepreneur, you already know that starting a business is a 24/7 job. Even when you're "off," you're not really off. You're thinking about how to grow the business, how to solve problems, how to make it better. If you want the easy way, get a nine-to-five job. It is much easier.

WEALTH MYTH #3: PASSIVE INCOME

Are you familiar with the idea of "passive income"? It was promoted in all those business books back in the 2000s. Just focus on passive income. Focus on getting money to come in automatically so you can retire. Network marketing companies love this idea. They sell people on the idea that by recruiting just a few people, they can sit on the beach and sip on mai tais as money rolls into their bank accounts.

Did you know that according to a Federal Trade Commission report percent of people who join a network marketing company don't make money? That's because anyone who joins focuses on passive income. Everyone wants to get something for nothing. The 1 percent who make money are not passive at all. How do I know? Some of my good friends are top network marketers. If they want to keep their "passive income," they continuously recruit people, attend conferences, fly to different hotels, run their team, and train new members. They are rarely sipping mai tais on the beach.

I realized there was something wrong with the concept. In most other areas of life, the idea of "passive" doesn't work. Let's say you decide to get fit. Would you say, "Hey, I want to get in shape. I'll do some passive exercises." No! That makes no sense. If you want a healthy relationship, you won't go on "passive dates."

The word "passive" has a dangerous meaning behind it. It implies that you can get something for nothing, and that's not how the world works.

Everything takes work. Even the most common passive income ideas—investing in stocks, selling products online, and buying real estate—all require some effort if you want to be successful at it. The market could change, and your stocks will be worthless if you don't do your research. When you're selling products, you're also putting time and money into marketing.

Even Richard Branson, Bill Gates, Warren Buffett, Elon Musk, and other wealthy people keep their wealth by actively engaging in their financial interests. They all work. They are all very active in their investments. They are all very busy in their business. Instead of the word "passive," which is very dangerous, I suggest using a different term: leveraged income. Leveraged income is income you generate by using other people's resources, time, and money.

When a start-up company raises capital from venture capitalists to fund them in the infancy stages, it is called leverage. When you hire employees and delegate tasks to them, that is leverage. When you use technology to automate manual tasks, that is leverage. You might ask,

What's the difference between passive and leveraged income? They sound pretty similar. Here's the critical difference: Passive income implies you get money for no work. Leveraged income is generated from leveraging other people's work. Leverage is an important concept to understand when talking about Scalable Businesses. For now, know that leveraged income trumps passive income.

WEALTH MYTH #4: FINANCIAL FREEDOM

For many people, the idea of "financial freedom" is having enough money so you don't have to work. It's having enough money so that you can do whatever you want, wherever you want, whenever you want. Sounds pretty good, right? The problem with this is that it's an illusion. I had a few automated businesses and investments that produced monthly revenue for me. If I did nothing, sales and revenue would continue to roll in. However, I soon found out that just because I have "financial freedom" today, it doesn't mean I'll have "financial freedom" forever.

Things change, markets change, economies change, government policies change. That means what may have given you "financial freedom" one day will provide you with nothing the next day.

Instead of financial freedom, I prefer financial confidence. It means knowing you have the skills and ability to make money, no matter what happens. It means you won't need to rely on a boss to give you a raise. It means you don't have to fear changes in the economy. It means you never have to feel at the mercy of external forces when it comes to your financial life. When you have financial confidence, it gives you real security, peace of mind, and comfort. That's what you should aim for in your career.

So how do you get that financial confidence?

THE CONCEPT THAT CHANGED MY LIFE: THE WEALTH TRIANGLE

This concept is simple but very profound—it is not theory or philosophy. It comes from my personal experience and observations. Daily, it's battle tested by clients, students, and fans from all around the world.

THE WEALTH TRIANGLE

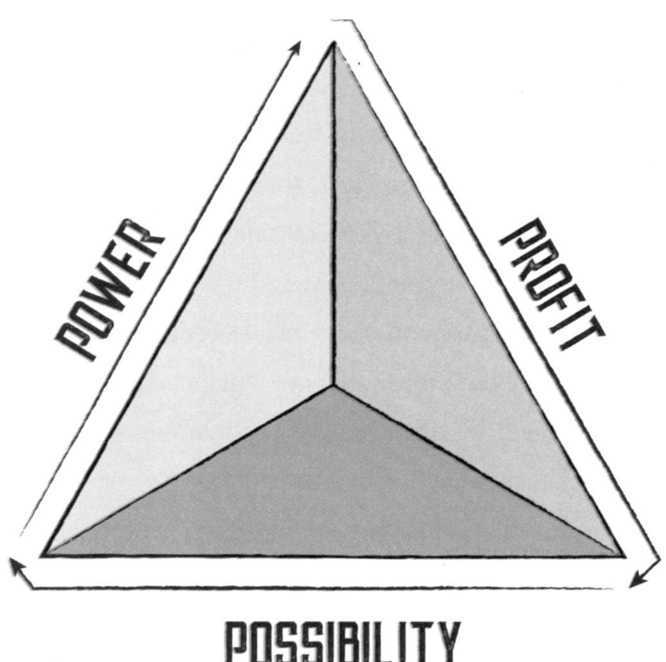

Here's how it works:

THE WEALTH TRIANGLE HAS THREE SIDES: POWER, PROFIT, AND POSSIBILITY

1. POWER COMES WITH HIGH-INCOME SKILLS

High-Income Skills allow you to earn $10,000 a month or more, providing a service other people know they need but do not know how to do themselves. It's a skill no one can take from you and is transferable across industries. In this case, you are trading your time for dollars. A High-Income Skill gives you income and comfort. It provides stability for your Wealth Triangle. With a High-Income Skill, you are taking back the POWER to control your life. You control your own time and your income. There's no more glass ceiling capping your income. The marketplace, not a boss, determines the value of your skill; this is true financial confidence.

If you're itching to learn more about High-Income Skills, you can jump to the chapter "Unlock Your High-Income Skills," where we dive deep into examples of High-Income Skills and how you can develop your skill.

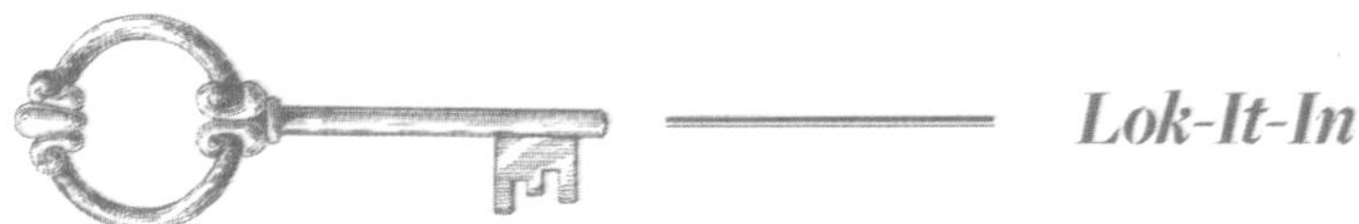

Lok-It-In

IT IS NO LONGER THE BIG FISH EATING THE SMALL FISH. IT IS THE FAST FISH EATING THE SLOW FISH. MONEY LOVES SPEED.

2. PROFIT COMES THROUGH SCALABLE BUSINESSES

A Scalable Business is a business you can repeat and grow with SPEED and WITHOUT a large amount of infrastructure or capital. For example, would a restaurant be a Scalable Business? No! Every time you want to open a new location, you need to invest time and capital resources and build new infrastructure. You would need to sign a new lease, invest more capital resources, renovate the place, hire new employees, train new employees, market the new location, and a million other things before it could run on its own.

A Scalable Business is a business you'll be able to grow to serve more customers without the overhead. For example, you don't need to create new offices to serve more customers with Uber or a SaaS. You will need to bring on more employees as you grow, but the number of employees you have won't cap your growth as much as it would if you were running a restaurant.

High-Income Skills provide you with a stable income, while your Scalable Business provides you with profits and cash flow.

3. POSSIBILITY COMES WITH HIGH-RETURN INVESTMENTS

A High-Return Investment is an investment that will provide you with a minimum 10 percent return, year in and year out. The purpose of the High-Return Investment is not to generate income. The purpose of the High-Return Investment is to grow your net worth and expand your POSSIBILITIES.

Your High-Income Skill gives you a stable income and helps you win back your POWER. With your Scalable Business, you are generating PROFITS. With your High-Return Investments, it builds your net worth and expands your POSSIBILITIES.

WHY THE WEALTH TRIANGLE BREEDS CLARITY

On the surface, the Wealth Triangle looks simple, and it is. When you look deeper, it answers many common questions that people have.

"Dan, I'm just getting started. What business should I start?"

None!

Don't start a business when you don't have any business acumen. Instead, focus on the High-Income Skill first. Learn to generate $10,000 a month first. You see people all the time on *Shark Tank* investing in what they think is a Scalable Business and sinking their life savings into it. "I came up with this amazing idea! So I put everything I had into it. I've mortgaged my house, borrowed from my family and friends, and now I've got two thousand board games in my garage. Invest in me!" And of course, if Kevin O'Leary were there, he'd reply, "You're dead to me."

HIGH-INCOME SKILL LINE

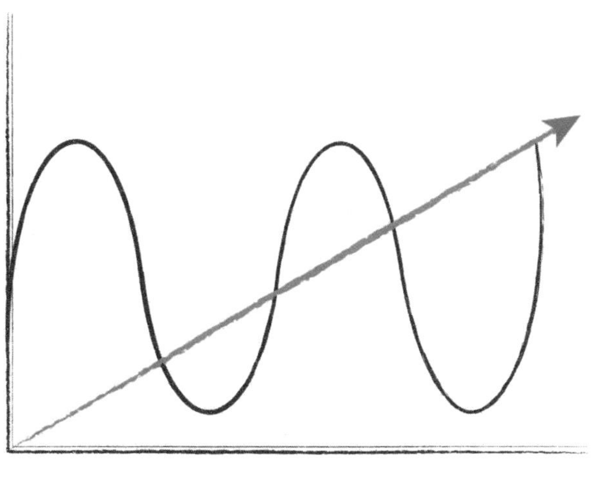

■ Business Cash Flow ■ High Income Skill

When you look at the previous graph, you'll see a black line fluctuating and a red line steadily rising. The black line represents the cash flow of a standard business. The red line represents the earning potential of a High-Income Skill.

As anyone who runs a business will tell you, the company has its ups and downs. Some years will be great; some years will be not so great. The cash flow fluctuates, which means you can't count on your business to be the foundation of your income. However, with a High-Income Skill, your earning potential does not change. It should grow every year. The reason it stays steady and grows is that your skill does not leave you, and because your High-Income Skill is transferable across industries, it is not as vulnerable to economic changes as a business.

Another question I often get is, "Dan, what should I invest in?"

Well, nothing if you have not developed your High-Income Skills. Why do you need to invest in anything? You need capital. If you want to invest in stocks, bonds, or cryptocurrency, you need money. If you don't have money, how can you keep reinvesting (even if you do find a good investment)? In the meantime, you also need to eat and pay the bills. Where will you get the money? The interests or dividends you get from the stock won't be enough—especially if you are starting out.

What about real estate? You probably know or have at least heard of people making money with real estate, right? Well, it's a different story if you are starting. If you buy the property and count on tenants to give you a monthly income, what happens if they move out? What happens if the toilet breaks? What happens when unexpected expenses come up? It'll most likely be much more headache than it's worth.

So before you jump into High-Return Investments, focus on developing High-Income Skills first.

CLARITY IS POWER

Hopefully by now you've gained a glimpse into why the Wealth Triangle is so powerful. It doesn't give one-size-fits-all advice; it acknowledges where you are in your current financial journey. What I am doing might not be the best action you can take, and what I'm investing in might not be the right fit for you. It all depends on where you are in the Wealth Triangle. When you understand the Wealth Triangle, you gain clarity. Clarity is power, and power is simply the ability to act.

We'll dive deeper into each component of the Wealth Triangle in the upcoming chapters. First, I want to introduce you to the six archetypes—six of the most common profiles today. Understanding your archetype will help you unlock your wealth, success, and significance much more quickly.

CHAPTER 2

Unlock Your Wealth Archetype

We all have different stories. You have your own set of unique experiences, beliefs, and ways of looking at the world. I have mine. However, we go on similar journeys. Over the past decade, I've spoken with millions of people around the world. They shared with me their stories, their journeys, and their transformations. Though each of them is unique and has different perspectives, I saw patterns emerging—patterns of common problems that stopped each person from achieving the next level.

These patterns are what I call "Wealth Archetypes." Once you know which Wealth Archetype you are, you'll know which of the following chapters in the book will be most useful to you.

THE SIX WEALTH ARCHETYPES

The Caged Lion

The Chained Magician

The Hustling Treasure Hunter

The Innocent Prisoner

The Successful Castaway

The Unfulfilled King/Queen

Let's jump in.

The Caged Lion

Picture this. You are a lion—fierce, wild, and born to hunt. You are the king of the jungle. Then one day you are blindsided by a group of hunters who tranquilize and capture you. Suddenly, you're inside a cage. You're angry, you're furious, and you want out. You roar the first few days and claw at the cage. You say to yourself, "I'm going to get out of here, and the minute I do, I'm going to show you how dangerous I am!"

As you roar and claw at the cage, you slowly get more and more tired. That's when the lion tamer comes in and throws you a piece of meat. You try to resist it because you're the king of the jungle; you don't need to be fed scrap pieces of meat. However, as time goes by, you get hungrier and hungrier. You need food to survive. You walk up to the meat and say to yourself, "I'll eat this one piece of meat, and that's it! Then I'll get out of here." But before you know it, the next day comes, and the lion tamer throws you the second piece of meat. Then the third day comes. You slowly become accustomed to living off of what's given to you. Instead of hunting, you become more and more reliant on the lion tamer. You live off of the scrap pieces of meat every day—meat that's enough to keep you alive, but never enough to make you full. You're not starving, but you're never truly satisfied either. When you rebel or start roaring, the lion tamer whips you and takes away your food. In order to stay alive, you have to start obeying the lion tamer, even though you know you could easily take his life.

A dangerous thing starts happening as time goes by; you get stuck in a routine. You wake up at the same time, you get food from the lion tamer at the same time, and you go to sleep at the same time. You are no longer hunting, no longer experiencing the thrill of life, and no longer the king of the jungle. Your prowess and hidden potential are kept trapped inside a cage. There's a voice screaming inside of you—frustrated, angry, and impatient. You are a LION; why should you have to listen to this lion tamer? You can go out and hunt on your own. All you have to do is step outside of the cage.

However, it's not that simple. There's also another voice inside your head, "I've been stuck in the cage for so long; do I still have what it takes to hunt?" You've been trapped in a cage for so long and gotten so used to the routine that you don't want to venture back out into the wilderness. Thoughts like, "What if I can't hunt anymore? What if I can't defend myself against other animals? What if I can't survive on my own?" run through your head.

The Caged Lion is the frustrated nine-to-five employee. They are the people who know they can "hunt" and provide for themselves, but they sacrifice that life in order for a predictable routine, even though the routine makes them miserable.

They listen to the "lion tamers"—their managers and bosses—who provide them with measly paychecks that are just enough to help them get by, but never sufficient to feast. In spite of how hard they work, hours they put in, or projects finished—they are stuck. Just like the Caged Lion, no matter how many tricks they can perform for the audience, they are thrown back into the cage at the end of the day. They are stuck in the life of sameness with no freedom. If the caged employee ever goes against the rules of the company or upsets their boss, they face punishment.

However, just like the Caged Lion, these people CAN hunt, and they CAN take down the lion tamer anytime they wanted to but are held back by fear of the unknown, fear of being inadequate, and fear of failure.

The Caged Lion has doubts about whether it can survive in the wild. The caged employee has doubts about whether they can survive without a steady paycheck.

> **Most of the people—they have fancy ideas in the evening. But when they wake up in the day, they go back to do the same job. We have to do something different.**
>
> JACK MA

The Caged Lion wants to ROAR and be king of the jungle. The caged employee wants to do bigger things than to repeat the same repetitive tasks for forty-plus hours each week. But what if I told you that the key to unlocking the cage is dangling from the lion tamer's waist—that it's right in front of you? What if I told you that the lion tamer looks down on you so much that they sometimes leave the cage unlocked, knowing that you don't have the guts to step out of the cage? Moreover, what if I told you that the hardest prison to escape is your mind? What if I told you that the only thing the Caged Lion has to do is build up the courage to step out of the cage and start hunting again? Caution is the major mistake the Caged Lion has made: the Caged Lion doesn't trust its hunting skills and instead trades it for the comfort of a predictable routine.

The Chained Magician

You are a powerful magician. You have powers most people can only dream about. Not only that, you are full of creativity, energy, and imagination. Your boundless energy allows you to think fast, learn fast, and act quickly. To you, the world has endless possibilities, and you say to yourself, "I can accomplish anything I set my mind to. If someone else has done it before me, then I can do it too. If no one has done it, then I'll be the first to do it!"

You know if you were permitted to use your powers, you could change the world; yet the village elders seem to suppress your powers. While you have these fantastic powers, the elders around you have prohibited you from using them. Why? So that other people in the village, who cannot use magic, won't feel threatened. Your magical powers are new and different—they would go against conventional wisdom. Even though your magic can bring about great change for your village, the elders value staying with tradition more than trying something new.

To keep the elders happy; you don't use your magic. You respect the village elders and everything they've done for you, but you feel chained, unable to use the full powers you KNOW you have within you.

The Chained Magician represents all the millennials and the new generation of talent who feel suffocated and pressured by their parents and society.

As a young and ambitious man or woman, you have all this energy and creativity inside of you. You KNOW you can change the world and create massive impact, but to keep your parents happy you are choosing to go the traditional route.

Have you heard any of these phrases before?

- *"Play it safe."*
- *"No one in our family has done this before."*
- *"You can't make a living doing that."*
- *"Get a degree, get a good job, get married, and buy a nice house."*
- *"What do you mean you're not getting a degree?!"*
- *"You've got to have a safety net."*
- *"Why can't you be more like them (your cousins, your friends, your siblings)?"*
- *"What if this doesn't work? Then what are you going to do?"*

- *"Why don't you get a job first and build up a safety net, and then you can do something riskier?"*
- *"If you don't get a degree, you're going to disgrace our family. You're going to be a loser. Companies won't hire you, and you're going to be out on the streets. Is that what you want?"*
- *"What am I going to tell our family and friends? That you're a dropout?"*
- *"Why are you so greedy?"*
- *"Why are you so ambitious?"*
- *"Don't stand out!"*
- *"Don't outshine other people; people will think you're arrogant."*
- *"Why can't you be happy with what you have?"*
- *"You have good benefits at your job; what if you can't find something better?"*
- *"We sacrificed so much for you so that you can get an education. We moved all the way here for you, and now you're throwing it all away?"*
- *"You used to be such a well-behaved and good kid; what happened to you?"*
- *"Don't you love me anymore? Why are you doing this to me?"*
- *"I did so much for you; why can't you just do this for me?"*

The worst part is that you're not following the traditional path for you; you're doing it for them. You know the traditional path won't get you to a place where you can give your family the life they want, so you feel chained, suffocated, and misunderstood. You say to yourself,

"Why can't they understand? I'm not doing this for me; I'm doing it for them. Why can't they support me? Why are they so negative? Why do they have to crush my dreams?" It's one thing if they don't understand, but it's another thing when they are actively sabotaging your goals and dreams. They make you feel guilty; they coax you into giving up; they want you to stop chasing your dreams, and all you can think to yourself is, "Why?"

Superman had this same conflict. He was born with all the power in the world, but his adoptive parents wanted to "protect him." They told him to dumb down his abilities, to hide them, to not let other people see his true capabilities. It's almost as if by trying to protect you, they are hurting you by holding you back. However, if you decide to release your power, you'll realize how much you can do, how much you're capable of, and how much impact you can have. Just like Superman, you'll need to make the same decision. Do you keep listening to your parents, or do you listen to your heart?

Remember, if you choose to go against your parents' suggestions, it doesn't mean you don't love them; it just means you love them in your way. They may not understand it now, but they will eventually. You might also feel alone and misunderstood right now, but as you go out and meet more people, you'll see there are more magicians just like you out there in the world. Once you shed the words of your elders and unleash your shackles, you'll start to realize you have more power than you could ever imagine, because that's the Chained Magician's biggest mistake. The Chained Magician believes their magical powers can be locked away by the words and opinions of their elders when, in reality, nobody can stop them but themselves.

If you decide to release your power, you'll realize how much you can do, how much you're capable of, and how much impact you can have.

The Hustling Treasure Hunter

The Hustling Treasure Hunter loves to go on adventures and find the next biggest chest of gold. They love the thrill of the chase, the allure of a new opportunity. They love going after the shiny objects in the sand. However, they like receiving new treasure maps more than they enjoy the actual search for the treasure chest. When they get a new treasure map, they'll excitedly announce to the world, "You wait! Once I find the hidden treasure full of jewels and gold, I'll be set for life! You'll be sorry that you missed out!"

However, as they follow the treasure map and realize it requires them to go through rough seas and uncompromising landscapes, they quit. They'll make excuses such as, "This treasure map was the wrong one. There's no treasure. This map lied to me. Don't worry—once I find the right treasure map I'll succeed for sure!"

The Hustling Treasure Hunter has the lottery mentality, believing external factors are what determines success, not internal factors. They borrow money and lose money on every failed venture. They put on a facade to pretend that things are going well, but deep down, they are terrified. They think to themselves, "Am I going to die at sea? Am I going to be killed by other pirates? Will the treasure I find even be enough to feed my family?"

These thoughts are too painful for them to think about, so they ignore them and continue to be distracted by the "chase." However, the life of the treasure hunter isn't glamorous either. They work very, very hard every day, but they have nothing to show for it. They have been traveling at sea for years without discovering treasure. Occasionally, they may find a tiny little bit of gold, but it's nothing significant. It may keep them afloat for a small amount of time, but it never gets them anywhere. It's never enough to get them out of the "treasure-hunter" lifestyle.

Meanwhile, their family is at home, wondering why they are never home, why they are always away. The treasure-hunter tells them, "Don't worry; this trip is the last one. I will find the treasure for sure, and then I'll have time to spend with you. Once we have the treasure, we'll have so much gold that we won't have to work at all for the rest of our lives!" However, this is never the case. The treasure-hunter is always on the hunt. They never find the "big chest of gold" that will allow them to escape the treasure-hunter life. The treasure hunter is lonely. Even when they team up to find treasure with other treasure hunters, they never feel like a team. Because all the treasure hunters are hungry to find gold, they will jump ship and switch teams as soon as there is a promise of gold with another crew.

Sooner or later, the Hustling Treasure Hunter finds out there is no loyalty in the world of treasure hunting. One minute, you think you are on a team united toward one mission. The next minute your team is jumping ship to join another crew of treasure hunters.

Who is the Hustling Treasure Hunter? Yep, they're the business opportunists.

These are the people who jump into the latest money-making schemes like Bitcoin, cryptocurrency, network marketing, drop shipping, day trading, etc. They will announce to the world that this opportunity is the "opportunity of a lifetime." These are the people who always post about how they're getting into a "ground floor opportunity" and to message them for more information. But three months later, you'll see them pitching something else. These are the people who have shiny-object syndrome. They are doing this at the same time they are doing that. They have a plan A, plan B, plan C, all the way up to plan Z.

If plan A doesn't work, they'll jump to plan B. If plan B doesn't work, they'll jump to plan C. While it appears things are under control, deep down inside they are scared to death. Now you might ask, Why do they have so many plans? The reason is not that they don't believe the ideas won't work. No. The real reason is that they say to themselves, "I don't believe I can make it work." Isn't that the truth? Can you think of people who have succeeded in real estate and people who have failed? Can you think of people who have succeeded in the stock market and people who have failed?

The truth is, it's not the plan that doesn't work—it's the person executing the plan. When someone doesn't believe in themselves, they will create backup plans, so they don't have to accept their failure. That's why they don't stick to any one thing long enough because they are too scared to focus or commit to one thing. They say to other people, "This time it's going to be different; this time it's going to work. Our family will be set." It is not long until they disappoint their family again; they'll dig their family further and further into a hole. They'll borrow money to join these crazy ventures. The allure of gold and profit sways them, but they'll fail every single time and have to go back to their family with another excuse.

The crazy thing is that the treasure was in their backyard the whole time—all they needed were the right tools to help them dig in their yard. You see, gathering "treasure" and gaining success is a lot like drilling for oil. The oil usually lies deep below the surface. To get to it, you'll need to invest a lot of time, effort, and energy. That means if you start drilling at one spot and you move on to the next place before you hit oil, all you'll end up with are shallow holes in the ground.

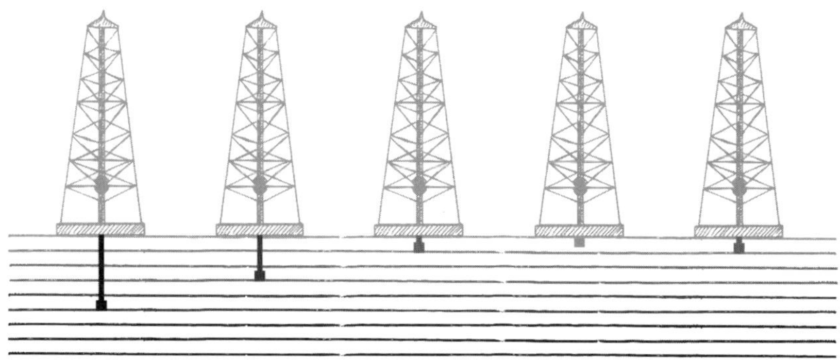

If you truly want to strike and hit oil, commit to one idea, and stick to it until you make results happen. When you stick to one thing and drill deep, you'll hit oil. You'll reach success. The Hustling Treasure Hunter does not do this. They are addicted to the chase because they don't believe they have what it takes to make it work. Until they fix what's inside themselves, things won't change. That is their biggest mistake.

The Hustling Treasure Hunter enjoys chasing many shiny opportunities but is too scared to commit to a specific one and quits before results can happen.

The Innocent Prisoner

What if you were jailed for a crime you didn't commit? How would you feel if all your life you had followed the rules, played by the books, and did everything "right" but somehow you still ended up in prison?

That's what an Innocent Prisoner has to go through. The Innocent Prisoner does everything by the book but somehow finds themselves trapped in a prison they cannot escape.

At a young age, these are the people who do well in school, get good grades, follow the rules, listen to their parents, and some even win scholarships. They work hard and make sacrifices. They're not afraid of hard work. Even after they graduate, they put in long hours at work to climb the corporate ladder. I'm talking about the lawyers, accountants, doctors, engineers—professionals who have followed the expected, conventional path. On the outside, they seem successful. They are in the middle class, are raising kids, and seem to have their life together. On the inside, however, they feel stressed, burned out, and empty. Some even take antidepressants to aid low-humming anxiety. They say to themselves, "I did everything I was supposed to do, so why do I feel lost and empty inside? What did I do wrong?"

They know that something is off, but when they mention it to friends or family they're met with questions like, "What do you mean you're not happy? You've got a great job, great house, and a great family. What could you be sad about?" They see other people taking risks and being happy, but they dismiss those people as being reckless. They've heard enough stories of people who venture out, go into business, and then go out of business. They don't want to be one of those people who fail. They make decent money, have a nice house, and live a quiet life. Everything is okay. But it's not a great life. This life has no adventure, no excitement, and no expression. They feel like there's a specific image of themselves that they need to uphold.

The worst part is that they don't think they can stop living this life because it would be irresponsible, even though deep down they're miserable. They bottle it up inside. They hide it, even from their loved ones. They justify it by saying, "I'm doing this for them. My happiness doesn't matter." The sad part is that their family wishes they would be more present at home. Because they are always working, they find it hard to be emotionally available. They spend all day working at a job they have to tolerate; of course, it's hard to connect when all they want to do is "turn it off." Soon enough, they'll wake up one day and think, "Where did the years go? They went by so fast." They force themselves to work extralong hours to maintain the status quo. They've seen other people at work laid off for no reason. They are under tremendous pressure, and they think to themselves, "What if I get laid off?"

This scenario is the Innocent Prisoner. They listened to others and believed it was the way to happiness. They built their prison brick by brick and threw out the key. The Innocent Prisoner's biggest mistake is believing that following conventional wisdom and rules will bring them happiness, instead of listening to their wants and needs.

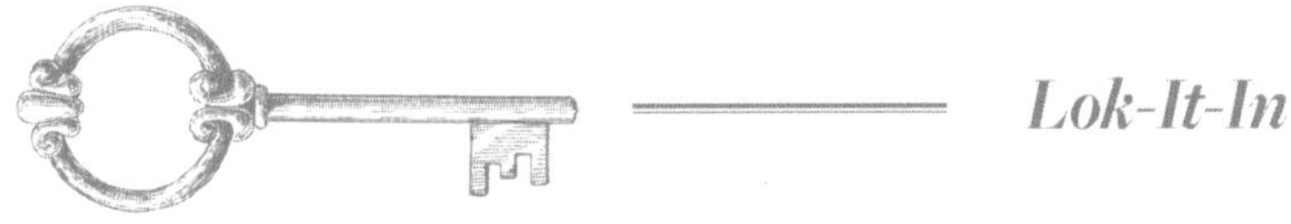

Lok-It-In

YOU CAN'T BECOME WHO YOU WANT TO BECOME BECAUSE YOU'RE ATTACHED TO WHO YOU'VE BEEN.

The Innocent-Prisoner In Real Life

A while ago, I came across a post on Reddit written by an intelligent forty-six-year-old man who lived the life of an Innocent Prisoner. It was touching and painted the struggles of an Innocent Prisoner perfectly. Summarizing it won't do it justice, so I'll share the entire post:

"Hi, my name's John. I've been lurking for a while, but I've finally made an account to post this. I need to get my life off my chest. About me. I'm a 46-year-old banker, and I have been living my whole life the opposite of how I wanted. All my dreams, my passion, gone. In a steady 9-7 job. Six days a week. For 26 years. I repeatedly chose the safe path for everything, which eventually changed who I was.

"Today, I found out my wife has been cheating on me for the last ten years. My son feels nothing for me. I realized I missed my father's funeral FOR NOTHING. I didn't complete my novel, traveling the world, helping the homeless. All these things, I thought I knew to be a certainty about myself when I was in my late teens and early twenties. If my younger self met me today, I'd punch myself in the face.

"Let's start with a description of me when I was 20. It seemed only yesterday when I was sure I was going to change the world. People loved me, and I loved people. I was innovative, creative, spontaneous, risk-taking, and great with people.

I had two dreams: writing a book and traveling the world.

"I had been dating my wife for four years by then. Young love. She loved my spontaneity, my energy, my ability to make people laugh and feel loved. I knew my book was going to change the world. I would show the perspective of the 'bad' and the 'twisted,' showing my viewers that everybody thinks differently, that people never believe what they're doing is wrong. I was seventy pages through when I was 20. I am still seventy pages in, at forty-six. By 20, I had been backpacking around New Zealand and the Philippines. I planned to do all of Asia, then Europe, then America (I live in Australia by the way). To date, I have only been to New Zealand and the Philippines.

"Now, we get to where it all went wrong—my biggest regrets. I was 20. I was the only child. I needed to be stable. I needed to take that graduate job, which would dictate my whole life. To devote my entire life in a 9-7 job. What was I thinking? How could I live when the job was my life? After coming home, I would eat dinner, prepare my work for the following day, and go to sleep at 10 pm, to wake up at 6 am the next morning. God, I can't remember the last time I've made love to my wife.

"Yesterday, my wife admitted to cheating on me for the last ten years. Ten years. That seems like a long time, but I can't comprehend it. It doesn't even hurt. She says it's because I've changed. I'm not the person I was. What have I been doing in the last ten years? Outside of work, I really can't say anything. Not being a proper husband. Not being ME. Who am I? What happened to me? I didn't even ask for a divorce, or yell at her, or cry. I felt NOTHING. Now I can feel a tear as I write this. But not because my wife has been cheating on me, but because I now realize I have been dying inside. What happened to that fun-loving, risk-taking, energetic person that was me, hungering to change the world? I remember being asked on a date by the most popular girl in the school but declining her for my now-wife. God, I was popular with the girls in high school, and college too. However, I've been loyal. I haven't taken time to explore. I studied every day.

"Remember all that backpacking and book-writing I told you about earlier? That was all in the first few years of college. I worked part-time and splurged all that I had earned. Now, I save every penny. I don't remember a time I spend anything on anything fun. On anything for myself. What do I even want now?

"My father passed away ten years ago. I remember getting calls from mom, telling me he was getting sicker and sicker. I was getting busier and busier, on the verge of a big promotion. I kept putting my visit off, hoping he would hold on. He died, and I got my promotion. I hadn't seen him in 15 years. When he died, I told myself it didn't matter that I didn't see him. Being an atheist, I rationalized that being dead; it wouldn't matter. WHAT WAS I THINKING? Rationalizing everything, making excuses to put things off. Excuses. Procrastination. It all leads to one thing, nothing. I rationalized that financial security was the most important thing. I now know that it is not. I regret doing nothing with my energy when I had it. My passions.

My youth. I regret letting my job take over my life. I regret being an awful husband, a money-making machine. I regret not finishing my novel, not traveling the world, and not being emotionally there for my son and being a damn emotionless wallet.

"If you're reading this, and you have a whole life ahead of you, please. Don't procrastinate. Don't leave your dreams for later. Relish in your energy, your passions. Don't stay on the internet in all your spare time (unless your passion needs it). Please, do something with your life while your young. DO NOT settle down at 20. DO NOT forget your friends, your family. Yourself. Do NOT waste your life or your ambition. Like I did mine. Do not be like me."

The Castaway

Imagine you are on an airplane, and it suddenly CRASHES. You wake up and realize you are alone on the shore of an abandoned island. What do you do? Of course, the first thing that comes to mind is to see if you can find others who are also stranded. You take a moment to gather your thoughts, and then you yell, "HELP! Is anyone here?" No response. You yell again—no answer. It's just you and the island.

You're thirsty, and you haven't eaten for what seems like days. There's no source of salt-free water nearby. Luckily, you find some fallen coconuts on the ground. You crack them open and drink the small bit of juice they had. These are the coconuts you'll later use to store water. What's the next step? You set up the shelter by using the washed-up lifeboat from the plane. Then you venture around the island to see if there are any signs of life. You find none. All you can see is the ocean surrounding the island. There are no other signs of land nearby.

Staring into the wide open, you realize that you are truly alone and must fend for yourself. You learn to catch fish and crab, but you can't eat it raw. You need fire. How in the world are you going to make fire? You take what you learned from Boy Scouts and start rubbing two sticks together. You rub the sticks for hours on end, but no results. You're getting frustrated. Suddenly, you push too hard on the stick, and it snaps in half. The sharp end slices part of your palm. You scream in frustration and anger and throw a washed-up volleyball against the trees. The volleyball comes back to you and the blood smeared on the volleyball vaguely resembles a face. In need of connection, you name this volleyball "Wilson." You now have a companion. (And yes, if you're wondering, this is the story of *Cast Away* featuring Tom Hanks.)

With your new companion, you try starting a fire one more time. This time some smoke appears. The smoke then turns into a spark, and that spark finally turns into a FIRE! You've created fire! Victory! You can now cook your fish and crab. You can finally eat. You wake up the next day and start hunting again since you can't preserve your food. You find a nearby water source and fill up your coconuts. This routine is how you live your life for the next year.

The Castaway is the struggling solo entrepreneur. You are starting your own business, but you feel alone. You have an entrepreneurial spirit, but there's no one around you who can appreciate it and share the journey with you. Every day feels like a struggle. You are hunting for food and water to survive the day. It feels as if you are always on a "feast and famine" cycle as you are either fulfilling on a client or trying to get new clients. When delivering work for a client, you feel safe knowing that when the invoice gets paid, you can afford to eat. When you are finding a job, it feels as if you'll starve.

Every accomplishment is difficult. Minimal achievements feel like a great victory. When you are just starting out, getting that first client feels like an impossible feat. Just like starting a simple fire on the island, your first client feels like a huge victory worth celebrating.

Even when you celebrate, there's no one really to celebrate with. It is hard for others to understand why you do what you do, so they stay away. So you go on your laptop and try to find connection—you try to find someone who will appreciate the accomplishment. However, just like Wilson, a laptop won't fill the void of a real-life human connection.

In a sense, you have "freedom" because you can do whatever you want to do, but you also lose the security of a predictable income. It's an income roller coaster, and you only eat what you kill. Just like the food on the island, the clients aren't sustainable. You can only gain income when you are delivering on the work.

On the island, the Castaway has to take care of their shelter, clothing, food, water, and protection. The solo entrepreneur needs to wear many hats—from marketing to sales to operations to customer support to accounting. Like a castaway, if you don't have a team or system yet in place to help lighten the workload, you do everything. While other people might think you are a business owner, you don't always feel like you are a business owner. You are not in control. While you are making a decent living, it's hard to imagine how this type of lifestyle could scale. Sometimes, you have to battle with imposter syndrome when you think to yourself, "When will they find out that

I'm not as great as they think I am?"

People think you can set your hours, and that's true in a sense, but the hours you set are 24/7. You think about your business all the time, and even when you are "off," you are still thinking about how to grow and sustain your business. The long hours, lack of security, and lack of a predictable income make you wonder, "How long will I have? Am I going to make it?" That is the life of the Castaway.

The Castaway's biggest mistake is living life as a lone wolf. While they have what most people consider "freedom," they are lonely, and they have no long-term sense of future certainty.

The Unfulfilled King/Queen

It wasn't easy, and you had to conquer many obstacles, but you're finally sitting on the throne. However, you didn't do it the easy way. No—you did it through conquest. You've worked hard for years or decades to get to this position, and now you have all that you've ever wanted: the fortunes, the lifestyle, and the status. You always knew you would get here; you've had the drive since you were young. All you had to do was work hard enough to get here. And you did.

However, for some reason, you were only happy for a few

moments when you took the crown—even though this was your lifetime goal. After the first moments of joy, your mind started feeding you unwanted thoughts: "What if someone tries to take my crown? What if they try to sabotage me? What if other kingdoms attack and try to take over our town?"

You now anxiously worry about how you could potentially topple. You identify your most significant threat. You see that the neighboring kingdom is building in strength and you think to yourself, "That's it! That's my next goal. I have to make sure they don't attack my kingdom so I can secure my crown." For most of next year, you prepare your army and plan for the attack. When you finally attack, you fight a hard-fought battle and end up victorious. Now, you have secured your crown, AND you have even more riches and respect than ever before. Everyone in the land recognizes you like the most dominant and skilled royalty. Then, "it" happens again. You feel joy for only moments and then start itching for the next achievement.

Does this Unfulfilled King/Queen sound familiar?

Yep, it's the overachiever.

As an overachiever, you were always the top of your class. Some people classify you as Type A, but you know how to work hard and succeed. You've been hustling your whole life and excelling your entire life. You might be a CEO, a talented executive, a senior partner, or some other high-up position. Whatever it is, you've worked your butt off to get to where you are. People in your field know who you are and respect you, and if they don't, they soon will. Like the Unfulfilled King/Queen, you have the money, the lifestyle, and the status, but you are always worried that someone is on your tail. You're worried that your peers will outperform you and strip you of the title that you worked so hard for. Your belief in life is that if you work hard, you'll have lots of achievement. If you have many achievements, you'll have lots of happiness.

However, this is not the case. Instead of achievement leading to happiness, overachievers get into a trap. The trap works like this: you work hard, the hard work turns into results, but as you achieve more, you see more shortcomings, not happiness. The shortcomings cause you to work harder, and then you achieve more, and then you see it makes sense that you operate in this way. After all, you did well in school and received plenty of praise from teachers and coaches as you were growing up. They made you feel like you were a part of a "special" group, better than everyone else. That type of upbringing does come with its consequences: you find it hard to be satisfied unless you are outdoing everyone else. As a wise man once said, "You can't win the race of fulfillment running on the track of achievement."

That's the biggest mistake made by the Unfulfilled King/Queen. They mistakenly try to find fulfillment through achievement instead of contribution.

WHICH WEALTH ARCHETYPES RESONATE WITH YOU?

- Are you the Caged Lion who only needs to trust his ability to hunt and step out of the cage?
- Are you the Chained Magician who is brimming with creativity, imagination, and magic?
- Are you the Hustling Treasure Hunter who could do much better by focusing on one opportunity instead of spreading themselves thin?
- Are you the Innocent Prisoner who has built their prison without realizing it?
- Are you the Castaway who is surviving alone on an island?

- Alternatively, are you the Unfulfilled King/Queen who is continually looking out for the next kingdom to seize?

Remember that the Wealth Archetypes are not set in stone. You can become a different archetype depending on the phase of your life as problems change with the passing of time, creating a need for different solutions.

You may be the Caged Lion right now, and you may become the Castaway later on in life—that's perfectly fine. What's important is that you are aware of your current situation. That way you can address your situation and its problems with the right solutions.

It's essential for you to identify your Wealth Archetype so you can see which of the following chapters will serve you best. Now that we know your Wealth Archetype, it's time to start exploring the appropriate High-Income Skill.

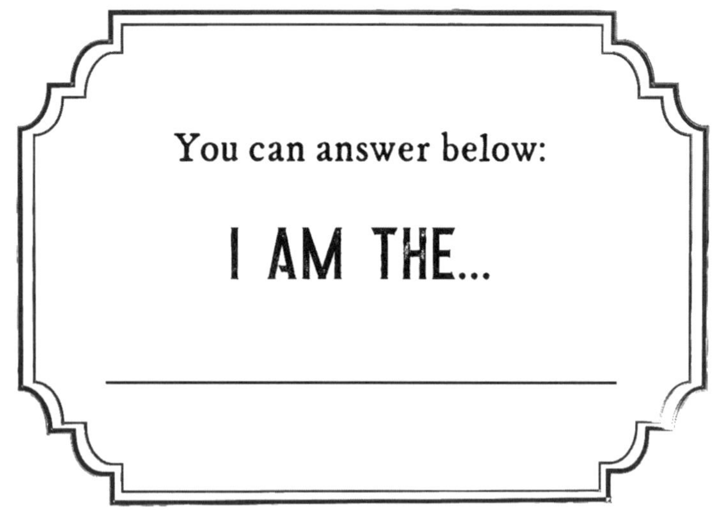

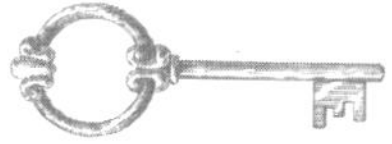

CHAPTER 3

Unlock Your High-Income Skill

IDEAL FOR: **CAGED LION, CHAINED MAGICIAN, HUSTLING TREASURE HUNTER, AND INNOCENT PRISONER**

Have you noticed that traditional jobs are disappearing faster and faster? Have you seen the news about technology and robots replacing more and more workers? Did you know that fewer and fewer workers can secure full-time jobs? If you look at the trends, you'll see the writing on the wall—the old way of working is disappearing.

In the past, you could graduate from college, land a secure job, work with the same company at the same job for forty years, and then retire at sixty-five. That's no longer the case, and you might already know that. Maybe you're starting your career, and you know there's no way you'll be staying at one company for forty years, or perhaps you've had to switch careers multiple times already, or maybe you know someone laid off recently and had to face the unforgiving job market.

Wherever you are at currently, you probably have a small hunch that something in the economy is changing. Well, you're right. The old "job economy" is steadily disappearing, and a new economy is emerging; it's what I call the Skill Economy.

THE EMERGING SKILL ECONOMY

TWO FACTORS ARE DRIVING THE NEW SKILL ECONOMY:

1. Fewer full-time jobs are available in the job market.
2. The available full-time positions are way too expensive for companies to keep.

Let's talk about the first one: there are fewer full-time jobs available than in the past. Have you seen the kiosks that are replacing cashiers at McDonald's? Have you ever spoken to an outsourced worker when you called into a call center? Haven't you heard the horror stories about companies going through "corporate downsizing"—you know, basically where they fire many people?

The world is changing. Regular full-time jobs are becoming less and less available. Companies are only keeping high-level executives and high-touch members as full-time staff—everything else can be automated, outsourced, or contracted. Not only that, but the full-time jobs that do remain are becoming too expensive for companies to keep.

"The US labor market is structured so that companies pay the highest taxes and offer the most benefits and protections for full-time employees, which means that hiring an employee can cost 30–40 percent more than equivalent independent workers."[1]

Now, if you were running a company, would you pay 30 percent more for an employee who does the same amount of work as another employee? Think about it in terms of your life. If you were buying a car, and two dealers offered you the same car—same brand, same model, same condition—and one dealer quotes you $20,000 while the other quotes you $26,000, which would you choose? Of course, you'd go with the $20,000 car, the less expensive option. This is the same decision many companies are now making.

With full-time jobs disappearing, contract work and freelance work are emerging, fueling the Skill Economy. People are being paid more and more based on their skills, not their credentials, experience, or job position. However, not all skills are created equal—some reward you better than others.

NOT ALL SKILLS ARE CREATED THE SAME

You're probably familiar with the concept of "supply and demand"—when there is high demand and low supply for something, it is more valuable; when there is low demand and high supply for something, it is less valuable.

It works the same way with skills. The principle of supply and demand divides skills into two categories: Low-Income Skills and High-Income Skills.

Low-Income Skills are high in supply and low in demand—that is why they will give you low pay. They are a commodity, and there are many more people out there who have these skills than there is a demand for them.

---

1 Diane Mulcahy, The Gig Economy (AMACOM16), 6.

As an example, imagine you are working as a cashier. There's nothing wrong with working as a cashier. It was my first and only job when I got started. I was paid minimum wage, and I had to work long, tough hours. I worked very, very hard, but my paycheck didn't reflect my efforts. Why was that? It's because working as a cashier is a Low-Income Skill. No matter how good or fast I was at ringing up the cash register, I could always be replaced by anyone on the street.

In contrast to Low-Income Skills, High-Income Skills are low in supply and high in demand—that's why they will give you higher pay. If you have a High-Income Skill, people will fight to hire you, because you can deliver high value.

Plus, if you have a High-Income Skill, the work you get will offer you much more compensation, flexibility, and happiness. In addition, you'll get the ability to control your finances, the time you work, and the location of your work. These are all crucial factors in deciding your happiness at work.

However, you might be wondering, "Dan, this all sounds good, but what exactly IS a High-Income Skill?" I'm glad you asked. If you look back earlier in the book, here's the definition for a High-Income Skill:

HIGH-INCOME SKILL

A skill that allows you to earn $10,000 per month or more, providing a service other people know they need, but do not know how to do themselves. It's a skill no one can take from you and is transferable across industries.

Let's take a look at each part of the definition to understand why it is defined this way.

WHY IS $10,000 THE MAGIC NUMBER?

There are two reasons why $10,000 per month is the magic number for a High-Income Skill.

First, by earning $10,000 per month (or $120,000 per year), you'll be in the top 6 percent of income earners in America. You'll be able to sustain a comfortable lifestyle—you'll be able to pay your bills, eat out at excellent restaurants, splurge a bit, and still have money left over to invest into you, a savings account, or your business. It gives you a peace of mind. It frees you from the stress of wondering if you'll have enough money for this month's expenses. Having that peace of mind AND having more "take home money" allows you to keep growing and expanding.

The second reason is a significant insight that no one else is talking about right now. It's an insight I've gained only from my personal experience. From my past two decades of teaching people from all over the world, I noticed something strange about people's psychology and income level. There's a "glass ceiling" most people have with earning $10,000 in a single month. If they don't make $10,000 a month, they are one type of person. If they DO earn $10,000 a month, they become another type of person.

I've seen people fluctuate between earning $2,000 to $9,000 a month as their income would go up and down like an income roller coaster. However, once they hit $10,000 in a single month, something shifts inside of them. They take on a new identity, a new comfort level, a new standard for what they will and will not accept in their life. They will do ANYTHING to stay at the $10,000 a month mark.

If they go below $10,000 in a month, they'll start to feel extremely uncomfortable and scramble to get back to where they were; this is something you won't see from someone who has never earned $10,000 in a month.

HOW TO BECOME IRREPLACEABLE

Remember that we said High-Income Skills are low in supply and high in demand; this means low-level skills like grocery shopping, mopping floors, and driving are NOT High-Income Skills. That's why people who work on apps like TaskRabbit or Uber won't likely make over $10,000 a month. There is nothing wrong with being an Uber driver. I think it's great for many people. It gives you flexibility and lets you earn outside of regular work hours. However, Uber drivers likely won't make a high income because they are replaceable. If one Uber driver isn't available, there were dozens of drivers waiting around the corner.

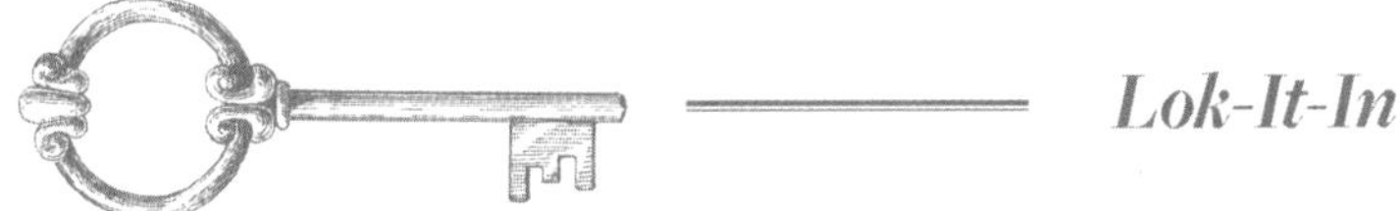

IT'S NOT HOW MUCH YOU EARN; IT'S HOW YOU EARN MONEY.

THREE DIFFERENT PATHS TO $10,000 A MONTH

There are many ways to earn $10,000 per month, but not all $10,000 incomes work the same way. HOW you make money could be just as important as the money itself.

Having Financial Confidence—the ability to earn money under any conditions, so we never have to worry about money again—is the goal.

There are three different ways to earn a high income: High-Income Job, High-Income Profession, and High-Income Skills. What's the difference?

1. HIGH-INCOME JOB

A high-income job is company dependent. The perfect example is climbing up the corporate ladder. You work hard and eventually move up to a middle-management or executive position. You're able to make $10,000 a month this way. However, there is one catch—what if your boss decides to fire you? Would you be able to take that same income to another company? Possibly, but it's not guaranteed. Would the position and status you had in one company be transferred over to the next? Again, possible—but not guaranteed. What if the company decides to implement "corporate restructuring"? What would you do then? Would your company knowledge be transferable to your job?

When you are at a high-income job, your income is determined by the company. They could demote you, fire you, or promote you, but it's mostly outside of your control (unless you want to engage in years of office politics). You're mostly a High-Income Slave.

2. HIGH-INCOME PROFESSION

A high-income profession is industry dependent. This profession is usually credentials based, meaning the more letters you have in front of or behind your name, the more you get paid. These are the doctors, lawyers, accountants, realtors, and dentists who study and work hard for six to eight years to get their education and degree. However, the pitfall of having a high-income profession is in its definition—it's industry dependent.

Can a podiatrist (foot doctor) become a dentist all of a sudden? Would you want someone who works with feet to fix your teeth? Probably not. If you're a Realtor and suddenly the market starts going into a downturn (as it always does in the economic cycle), what do you do? You're as good of a Realtor as before, but what changed? Nothing—except the market and the economy. None of which are within your control. When that happens, you have to work way harder to maintain your current income.

On top of all that, many High-Income Professions are location dependent. If you are a dentist, Realtor, lawyer, or any profession, you usually operate out of your office, and your clients/patients are generally local. Let's face it: if you're a dentist, not many people are going to drive thirty miles to see you, no matter how good you are. That's why I teach High-Income Skill development.

3. HIGH-INCOME SKILL

High-Income Skills are limitless. A High-Income Skill gives you the most freedom because what you are worth is only capped by how much value you can bring to the marketplace. It is not company dependent because you can go to another client who will want your service. It is not industry dependent because a High-Income Skill works across all industries. It's not location dependent because a High-Income Skill does not require your physical presence as long as you can deliver value to your customers. With the advancements in technology, it's easier than ever to work from home, a coffee shop, or anywhere you'd like.

Once you acquire your High-Income Skill, you'll be able to start living your life with real financial confidence.

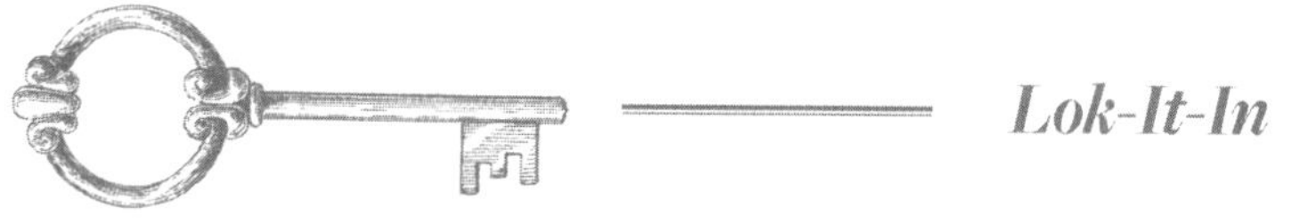

JOBS GET YOU NOWHERE. PROFESSIONS GET YOU SOMEWHERE. SKILLS GET YOU ANYWHERE.

UPGRADE YOUR SKILLS, UPGRADE YOUR INCOME

Let's look at a High-Income Skill like High-Ticket Closing®. With High-Ticket Closing®, you get a commission for every deal you close. So if you close a $3,000 sale and your commission is 10 percent, you receive $300. You can earn $3,000 a month by closing ten deals. Let's say you closed ten deals after taking one hundred calls that month, so you closed one out of ten calls. But what if you get better at your skill? What if you practiced more, read more books, or got more coaching?

What if instead of closing one out of ten, you closed two out of ten? Instead of closing ten deals a month, you would now be closing twenty sales a month. At $300 for every commission, you wouldn't be getting $3,000 next month—you would be getting $6,000. That's the power of having a High-Income Skill—your income rises as you become better at your skill.

CAN HIGH-INCOME SKILLS MULTIPLY YOUR INCOME?

When you "stack" your High-Income Skills correctly, they can amplify each other and multiply your income. Let's say you have one High-Income Skill earning you $10,000 a month. If you can stack another High-Income Skill on top of that, you can make another $10,000 per month with a little amount of work and effort added.

Let me tell you my story of stacking High-Income Skills. Alan, my mentor, taught me my first High-Income Skill of copywriting. If you ever watched *Mad Men*, you'll know that copywriting is salesmanship in print, an essential skill for creating successful marketing promotions. With copywriting, I was able to open up my own "one-man ad agency" and made $10,000 a month. Now, if this were a high-income job, my income would be capped here, and that's all I would be able to make. I was taking on many clients at once and working long hours to fulfill the orders, so I couldn't increase my income by adding on more work. However, because I was able to stack my High-Income Skills, I could add to my income.

You see, as I worked with more and more clients, they started asking me questions about how to use the marketing promotions I wrote for them. "Dan, this is a great piece of work you've done for us, but how do I use it effectively?" So in addition to writing the promotions for my clients, I started teaching them how to use my work. I showed them how to promote it, where to promote it, and what to expect when they launched the campaign. It wasn't much additional work, just an hour or two here and there, but that allowed me to increase my income by another $10,000 a month. That was how I got my second High-Income Skill of consulting.

Without adding too many extra hours, and by working with the same clients, I doubled my income; I went from $120,000 to $240,000 per year. Are you starting to see the power of stacking High-Income Skills?

HIGH-INCOME SKILL STACK

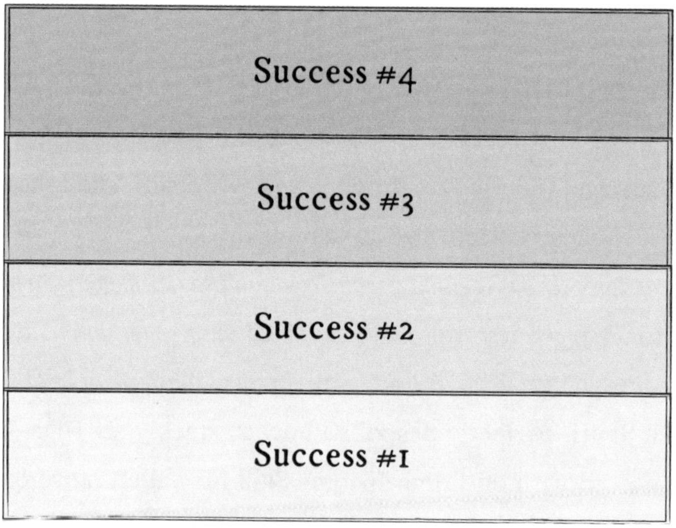

Success #4
Success #3
Success #2
Success #1

Not only that, I added another High-Income Skill to my stack—the skill of High-Ticket Closing®.

High-Ticket Closing® is the unique skill of closing deals that are valued at $3,000 and beyond. These are large transactions that require human interaction to complete. In my "one-man ad agency," I was making a good living just by offering my copywriting and consulting services. However, I knew that if I wanted to rise to the next level of income, I had to start working with clients who were paying top dollar. With the skill of High-Ticket Closing®, I landed larger clients who were willing to invest a premium price for premium results. By allowing me to work with "bigger fish," High-Ticket Closing® was the High-Income Skill that moved me to the next level of income.

Then, I added one more High-Income Skill: digital marketing. By leveraging the reach of the online world, I could reach massive amounts of people and deliver more value to more people. That's how I was able to go from earning $100,000 to earning millions by stacking one High-Income Skill on another. Sounds simple, and it is—but it's not easy.

THE NUMBER-ONE MISTAKE PEOPLE MAKE WHEN DEVELOPING THEIR HIGH-INCOME SKILL

A few years ago, Charlie Rose interviewed Will Smith and asked about his secret to success. Here's what he replied:

"You don't set out to build a wall. You don't say, 'I'm going to build the biggest, baddest, greatest wall that's ever been built.' You don't start there. You say, 'I'm going to lay this brick as perfectly as a brick can be laid.'"

Will Smith perfectly described how to stack your High-Income Skills: succeed with one High-Income Skill first, then move onto the next. This way, you'll build a High-Income Skill stack. Most people develop High-Income Skills in the wrong direction. They will try one skill for a while, and then jump to the next, and then jump to the next before even developing slight competency with their current skill. Instead of building a wall like Will Smith described, they are making a brick pile.

HIGH-INCOME SKILL PILE

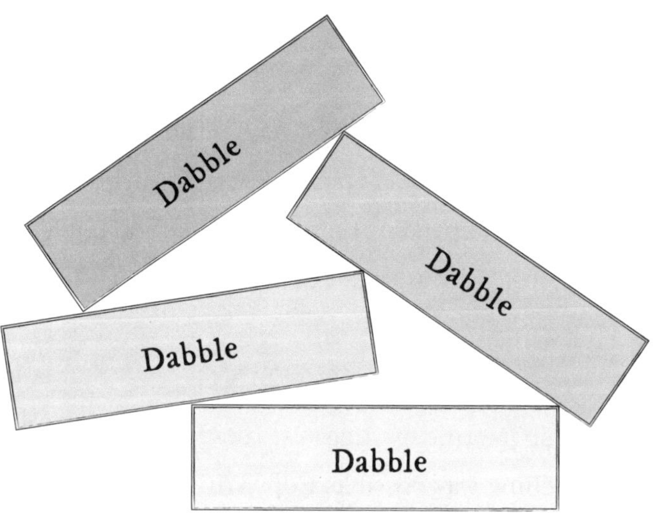

You may go through times that are tough when developing your High-Income Skill. Maybe you'll reach a plateau, or perhaps you'll struggle with finding people who will pay for your skill. The mistake I see people make too often is abandoning the High-Income Skill they have been working on when results don't come quickly. My advice for people who want to change course: be patient. Wait until you can earn $10,000 a month with your first High-Income Skill before moving to the next.

$120,000+ HIGH-INCOME SKILLS (NO DEGREE REQUIRED)

Your next question might be, “Okay, I get it. High Income-Skills are the way to go. So which one should I pick?” The right High-Income Skill for you will be different depending on what you like and don’t like, but to give you some ideas, here are a few of my favorite High-Income Skills.

COPYWRITING

It is salesmanship in print: crafting ads, sales letters, and sales pages in the most compelling way possible. Copywriting is arranging words to make a product sell better. If you’ve seen a billboard, a newspaper ad, a Facebook ad, or any Super Bowl commercial—that’s copywriting. Heck, if you’ve written a text to get someone on a date, that’s copywriting! It is one of the best High-Income Skills to develop. It’s the one that I started with first.

CREATIVE WRITER

Creative writing encompasses everything from ghostwriting, freelance writing, blogging, and much more. It is incredibly lucrative for creative minds and free thinkers.

CONSULTING

A consultant is a creative problem solver who can look at a business from an objective view. They look at a problem and present a solution. In essence, consultants trade their expertise for money. A good consultant provides unbiased advice and expertise. If you have something you are good at doing, something your friends always come to you for help with, or an area in which you know you excel, then you may have a start to a consultancy business.

DIGITAL MARKETING

Digital marketing includes mapping out funnels, managing Facebook pages and ads, growing Instagram accounts, building customer relationships, and more. Digital marketing is a massive opportunity for young and ambitious people who are already familiar with social media. If you love social media, why not choose it as a High-Income Skill? With the boom of social media, companies can't keep up with the trends. If you can learn this skill and take on four $2,500/month clients, that's your High-Income Skill right there.

BLOGGING/CONTENT CREATION

Blogging is similar to creative writing, but if you have an independent blog, you can learn how to manage online marketing, run ads, drive traffic, and much more. It is an excellent High-Income Skill if you can create valuable content that helps other people. If you can combine excellent writing skills with marketing skills, you could be well on your way to making blogging your next High-Income Skill.

NEGOTIATION

Negotiation skills are essential for just about everything. Though you may not be paid for $10,000 a month for this alone, it amplifies everything else you do. Whether it's negotiating with clients, potential partners, or vendors, the negotiation could make or break the deal; this is one of the most critical High-Income Skills that makes all of your other High-Income Skills more effective.

PUBLIC SPEAKING

More people fear public speaking than death. That means at a funeral, more people would rather be in the casket than delivering the eulogy. That's why a very select few people have truly mastered this one. It's not just being able to speak confidently in front of a crowd—it's about communicating a story and a vision to the audience.

LANGUAGE TRANSLATION

With the rise of globalization, countries from around the world are starting to do business with one another. If you are fluent in multiple languages, then this would be a tremendous High-Income Skill to develop. Learning a language is not something most people can do in a short time. That's why most will pay someone else to do it.

PHOTOGRAPHY

I have a friend who is a high-end photographer who gets paid handsomely for his work. However, he is not just the "photo guy." He works with his client to make sure he understands their needs and offers suggestions for shots that will capture the experience forever. It's this type of care and empathy that allows them to charge high end prices.

PROGRAMMING

Technology is becoming more and more pervasive in our world. Soon (and even now), AI and VR will play a massive part in our society. Programmers are needed in all industries—from marketing to health to finance. If you're extremely analytical and programming suits your goals—go for this as your High-Income Skill.

HIGH-TICKET CLOSING®

High-Ticket Closing® is the ability to close high ticket sales. While most salespeople focus on getting the deal, High Ticket Closing® is all about meeting the prospect's needs and letting them make their own educated decision.

When companies want to sell products/services that are $3,000 and beyond, it usually requires another person on the phone, as these aren't transactions that can be done through simple order forms online. That's where High-Ticket Closing® comes in.

It's also an invaluable skill for anyone who has their own business. If you have a business, you likely want to charge more for what you are currently doing. Without the skill of High-Ticket Closing®, you usually can only compete on price. If you win the competition of being the cheapest in the market, you don't win at all.

High-Ticket Closing® is one of my favorite High-Income Skills that I have taught to students from over 150 countries. You'll learn more about it in chapter 7—Unlock Your Sales. There you'll find an in-depth guide on how to close High-Ticket Deals over the phone.

THE ULTIMATE HIGH-INCOME SKILLS

All of these examples have the potential to become High-Income Skills, but there are three High-Income Skills that I love: High-Ticket Closing®, copywriting, and digital marketing. They're the ultimate High-Income Skills because they help other businesses generate revenue or acquire new customers.

These High-Income Skills are recession proof, have the highest earning potential, and companies will always need these High-Income

Skills regardless of how the economy is doing. When the economy is doing well, companies want more customers. When the economy is doing poorly, companies need more customers. Either way, people with these High-Income Skills are always in demand. Guess what? It will never go out of style. Artificial intelligence and robots won't ever take it down because some transactions still need a human touch.

You might think, "But, Dan, I'm not a salesperson or marketer. How does this apply to me?" The great thing about this is it's a learnable skill. I've trained tons of people from all walks of life, and most of them aren't salespeople. It's like riding a bike. Do you remember when you first learned to ride a bike? It's scary at first, and you fall a few times, but as you get better at balancing on two wheels, it becomes fun. Once you learn it, you keep that skill for life. You never forget how to ride a bike. It's the same with these High-Income Skills.

HOW DO YOU DEVELOP YOUR HIGH-INCOME SKILL?

Now that you understand the power of having a High-Income Skill, doesn't it make sense to develop one yourself? First, you should know what stops most people from getting their High-Income Skill. It is not the lack of information or resources; it's something much deeper than that.

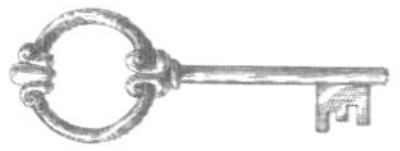

CHAPTER 4

Unlock Your Luck

The number four is bad luck in Chinese culture—so we are going to skip this one.

CHAPTER 5

Unlock Your Personal Power

IDEAL FOR: **CAGED LION, CHAINED MAGICIAN, INNOCENT PRISONER, HUSTLING TREASURE HUNTER, CASTAWAY**

What exactly is holding people back?

My whole life, I've been obsessed with finding out the answer to this question. Why are some people more successful than others? It seems that we all have the same capabilities, yet most people don't accomplish what they want to achieve.

When I hear some people say, "I can't do it," I wonder, "Does that mean you don't know how to do it? Or you don't want to do it?" Because we all have the power to make something happen—so is it a lack of knowledge, or is it a lack of will? Most people think what holds them back is the lack of knowledge. The first thing they do when they're not getting a result is to look for "how to" do something. They search for "how to lose weight," "how to start a business," "how to get a raise," "how to get promoted," how to do this, how to do that.

Let's look at an example. Do you know what the keys are to losing weight?

When people look up how to lose weight, they'll find dozens of different diets, each promising it will help you lose weight. There's the keto diet, Atkins diet, vegetarian diet, vegan diet, Weight Watchers diet, raw food diet, and on and on and on. But when it comes down to losing weight, don't we all know what it takes to lose weight? We know it pretty much boils down to two things—eat less and move more!

We all know what we need to do, but why don't we do it? Why do we procrastinate when we're fully aware of what we need to do? So maybe the problem isn't that we don't know what to do; maybe the problem is not doing what we know.

Isn't it true? The problem is not a lack of knowledge. If you want to lose weight, get promoted, start a business, or do ANYTHING, all you have to do is a quick internet search. How many podcasts, books, blogs, articles, and courses will you find? Chances are you'll find millions upon millions of hits. You could spend thirty years reading through the information from a single search result and still not be finished.

In many cases, there is way too much information and "how to" advice. People get paralyzed—they freeze, they analyze, they don't act—and that's what holds them back. The reason they don't act is not from a lack of knowledge—it's because they have access to too much knowledge.

Most people are drowning in knowledge yet starving for wisdom.

There is plenty of information on how to achieve any goal. Lack of knowledge is not the problem. Lack of wisdom is.

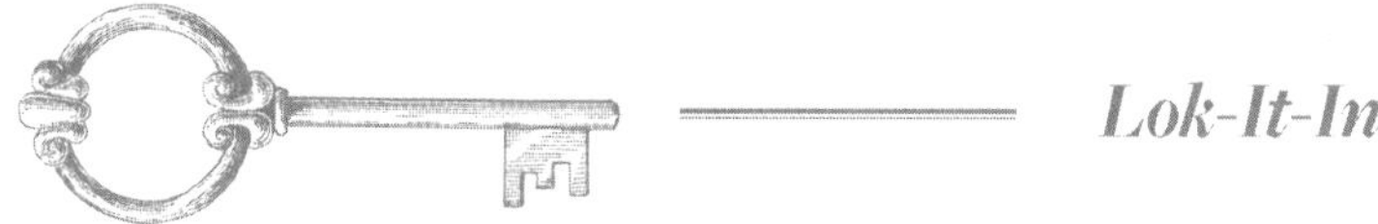

Lok-It-In

MOST PEOPLE ARE DROWNING IN KNOWLEDGE YET STARVING FOR WISDOM.

WHY WE NEED LESS KNOWLEDGE AND MORE WISDOM

Knowledge gives you the potential for taking action. Wisdom gives you the power to turn your knowledge into action.

Knowledge is about knowing what to do. Wisdom is knowing what doesn't need to be done.

Knowledge is abundant. Wisdom is scarce.

Too much knowledge will give you confusion, but the right amount of wisdom will provide you with power.

Too much knowledge will get you stuck, but the right amount of wisdom will get you unstuck.

> We can't solve problems by using the same kind of thinking we used when we created them.
>
> ALBERT EINSTEIN

WHAT TO DO WHEN YOU'RE STUCK

You see, when you are stuck in life, what you think is the problem is usually not the real problem. So the real solution often lies outside of what you already know. Let me show you what I mean.

Let's imagine that there is a box. Inside this box is "what you know."

Your ego, your experiences, and all your existing current beliefs live inside this box. For most people, this box is tiny and compact.

Now, imagine there's another larger box around the "what you know" box. This box represents "what you don't know."

Notice how this box is much bigger. There is a lot more of what you don't know than what you do; however, it gets even more interesting. Now I want you to imagine a LARGE area outside of both boxes.

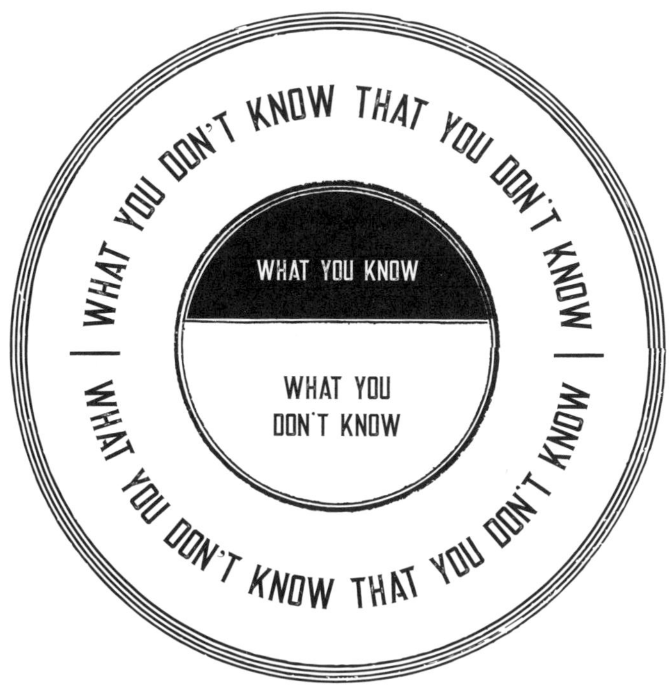

This space represents "what you don't know that you don't know."

See, most people don't know what is holding them back. They focus on learning more and gaining more knowledge because they say to themselves, "Once I know how to do X or Y, then I'll be successful." In reality, they are being held back by invisible forces that they aren't even aware are impacting them. That might sound confusing right now but stay with me. I'll give you an example.

Imagine you are driving a car. You push on the gas pedal, and the vehicle begins to move forward. Suddenly, the car slows down, and you have no idea why. You think to yourself, "I must not be pressing on the gas pedal hard enough; I'll just step harder." So you step on the gas, but the car is still moving at a snaillike pace; this is what most people do when faced with problems. When something is not working, their solution is to "work harder"—press on the gas pedal a little bit harder.

However, most people don't realize that pressing on the gas pedal is not always the right answer. Sometimes, people don't understand that their EMERGENCY BRAKE is on! Now think about what happens when you release the emergency brake. Wouldn't you surge forward with blazing speed? For people always struggling with the same problems, this is their problem. It's not that they are not working hard enough; it's just that they have their "emergency brakes" on.

What are these "emergency brakes"? They are the invisible forces that hold you back—what I call "Invisible Chains." After teaching tens of thousands of people in person and tens of millions online, I found that every person has at least one of these "Invisible Chains" holding them back from achieving their goals.

Sometimes these chains are hidden in plain sight and seen as "normal" by society, but when you put them under scrutiny, you'll see how limiting they become. Sometimes these chains are subconscious beliefs instilled into us at a young age to help us to blend into society, but if we want to stand out and live a life of success and significance, these beliefs hold us back. Sometimes these chains are just part of the age and the environment we live in at the moment. They seem like a part of everyday life, so we don't question it.

See if you recognize some of them.

THE SEVEN INVISIBLE CHAINS

INVISIBLE CHAIN #1: "GET RICH SLOWLY"

Why do you want more money? Sure, you might want to buy more things, but what about after that? You probably want to escape your job if you hate it. You probably want to spend more time with your family, spend more time doing what you enjoy. You probably want to travel and indulge in new experiences. You want more TIME for what you want in life. Most people think that wealth is measured by the amount of money you have. It's not. It's measured in time. The faster you can earn your money, the wealthier you are. Let me prove it to you.

Let's say you make $25,000 a year, and you do this for forty years, how much have you made?

$25,000 x 40 years = $1,000,000

Yes, a million dollars is a LOT of money. The problem isn't that you made a million dollars; the problem is that it took you forty years to do it. Instead of doing it in forty years, what if you made a million dollars in one year? Would you have made the same amount as before? Yes, except this time, you made it forty times faster. You are forty times wealthier than the person who makes it in forty years.

That's why wealth is measured more in time than money. So if you want to become wealthy, it's better to do it quickly than to do it slowly.

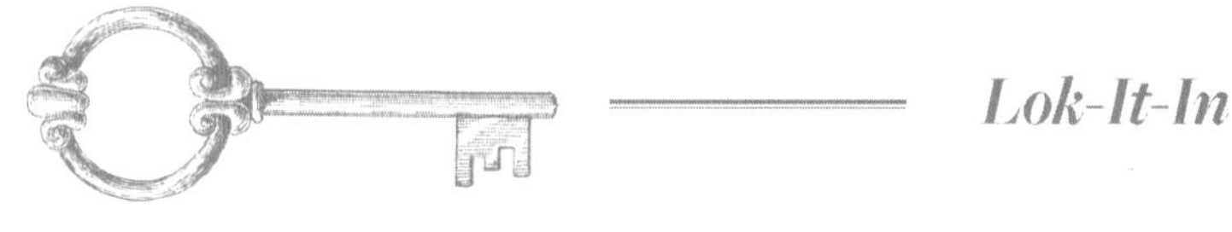

Lok-It-In

WEALTH IS MEASURED MORE IN TIME THAN MONEY.

When most people think of the idea of "getting rich quick," or if you even mention the idea, they think it must be some scheme or scam, or it must be something shady. In fact, "getting rich quick" is the only way to do it because wealth is measured in time, not money. This connection is one of society's Invisible Chains. It doesn't mean you can make it without effort. You still need to work hard. The difference is that some people work very hard for forty years and they're STILL not able to retire comfortably. Money earned is a by-product of value creation.

Value Delivered x People Served = Money Earned.

If you want to earn more money, you can either deliver more value to the same amount of people or provide value to more people. Neurosurgeons get paid well because they give a very high-value service to their patients. Influential entrepreneurs like Mark Zuckerberg, Steve Jobs, and Elon Musk are also paid well—because their work offers something of value that touches billions of lives. So, the question to ask if you want to earn more money is, "How can I deliver more value to more people?"

When you have a High-Income Skill, your income growth is exponential. You can deliver more value and help more people with your skills, making it possible for you to make more money more quickly. You're paid in direct proportion to the value you bring to the marketplace, not by how many hours you work.

CHAIN BREAKER: MONEY LOVES SPEED.

INVISIBLE CHAIN #2: YOUR CURRENT SELF-IMAGE

"You can't become who you want to be because you're too attached to who you've always been."

Do you know a couple that's been together ten, twenty, maybe thirty years and still have that spark, passion, and fire in their relationship? On the other hand, do you know people who've been a couple for only a short while, yet they want to strangle each other?

Do you know someone happy and positive, even when things are going wrong? In contrast, do you know someone who is always complaining and grouchy, even when everything is going right in their life?

The reason behind all of this is one of the most significant psychological discoveries of our century—it's the concept of self-image. I shared this concept in one of my TEDx Talks. You see, you and I have an image of ourselves. What you see in the mirror reflects your physical being, but that's not how we see ourselves—that's not our self-image. To see your self-image, all you have to do is look at the aspects of your life. Look at your body, your position at work, your love life, your current income. These are all outward expressions of your inner self-image.

Your self-image is what you consider to be appropriate for you; it's what you can see yourself doing or achieving. Most people attempt to change their body, finances, relationships, or income by changing something outside of themselves when the problem lies within. Self-image becomes a self-fulfilling prophecy.

That's because the strongest force in human personality is the need to remain consistent with how we see ourselves.

If you see yourself as conservative and safe, would you do something like bungee jumping or skydiving? If you see yourself as outgoing and sociable, would you stand alone by the wall at a party? On the other hand, if you see yourself as introverted and shy, would you introduce yourself to every stranger at a party? Most of us have trapped ourselves in an old self-image—in expectations of what we believe is possible for us.

Most of our self-image is picked up early in life from the people around us: family, siblings, friends, teachers, the media, society, and authority figures. Simple phrases like "You're so shy" or "You're such a troublemaker" can have a huge impact on us growing up because we believe everything we're told when we are young. The problem with this is that our self-image may not always align with what we want in life. Often when we try something new, we face much internal resistance. We feel like "this is not me."

We all have the urge to remain consistent with how we see ourselves. That's a huge part of why you don't act on the knowledge you already know. Because you don't do what you know, you do what you are. You act according to your self-image. Do you know what's sad? Sometimes people will lower their self-image to match their circumstances. Life has beaten them down over and over again, and before you know it, they give up. They stop trying to make their lives better. They say to themselves, "I guess that's just the way it is." Instead of raising their standards, they lower their expectations to meet their current reality. Luckily, it works the other way too. When you improve your self-image, you will feel an incredible urge to achieve more. Once you improve your self-image, your actions will follow.

HOW TO CREATE GREAT HABITS WITHOUT MOTIVATION

Years ago, I had a friend named Mike. He would always be up at 6:00 a.m. and would run for an hour. Nothing stopped him from his morning routine. One day, I asked him, "Mike, how do you have so much discipline and motivation to run every morning? What is your secret? You never miss a day!"

Mike gave me a weird look and said, "Dan, I run because I'm a runner."

He said it as an undeniable fact. He didn't tell me that he listened to motivational tapes every day. He didn't have to schedule in his runs; he didn't have to hire a running coach. He was a runner. The source of his motivation didn't come from discipline. The source of his motivation came from his self-image.

When you have a strong self-image, strong habits will follow. If you have healthy habits but a weak self-image, you'll always revert to your poor self-image. Isn't that why some people gain all their weight back after losing it? It's not that they didn't follow their diet and exercise plan. It's that they saw themselves at a certain weight, and their reality met their expectations.

HOW TO GET THE CAR OF YOUR DREAMS

When I was starting to rise in my career, I had a dream car in mind, the Mazda RX-8. I knew what I wanted—the modifications, the add-ons, the color. I knew down to the cent how much I needed to invest in this car. The problem was that it was way out of my price range. However, I didn't lower my standards by saying, "You know what, this other car is kind of what I want, and it fits my budget more; maybe I'll take that one." No. I wanted the Mazda RX-8, and I was going to get it. No other car would do.

I could picture myself driving the car and imagined how the steering wheel would feel in my hands. I visualized getting into the car. I imagined the smell of the leather seats. In my mind, I saw everything down to the last detail. To make it even more real for me, I went to the dealership and asked to test-drive the car, even though I couldn't afford it. I did it just to know how it felt to drive the car. I did this multiple times. (Of course, I had to go to different dealerships or else they would've probably kicked me out.)

The point is, in my mind, I already owned the car. Whenever I saw the car on the road, I would point to the car and tell my friend, "That's my car."

"What do you mean?"

"You see that RX-8? That's my car."

"What are you talking about? You don't have a car like that."

"You'll see. That's my car."

My friend just looked at me like I was crazy and changed the subject.

Eventually, I was able to get the car. I went into the dealership, pointed to the car I wanted and bought it right on the spot. The dealer later told me it was the fastest sale he ever made. How do you think I felt after getting my RX-8? Most people would think that I must have felt amazing after working so hard and waiting so long to get it.

I felt nothing.

I felt like I would any other day because I had driven the car in my mind many times. It was almost as if I already owned the car long before I bought it. Conventional wisdom says, "I'll believe it when I see it." That's not how it works. You have to see your dreams first, live as if they're already a reality, and THEN they will come true. So instead of lowering your expectations to meet your current reality, live your life as if all your dreams have come true and then challenge your reality to catch up.

CHAIN BREAKER:
LIVE YOUR LIFE AS IF ALL YOUR DREAMS HAVE COME TRUE AND THEN CHALLENGE YOUR REALITY TO CATCH UP.

INVISIBLE CHAIN #3: NEGATIVE FRIENDS AND FAMILY

One day, a gentleman walked along the beach and saw a fisherman who had crabs in the bucket. However, the bucket did not have a lid. Confused, the gentleman asked the fisherman, "Excuse me; aren't you afraid that the crabs will crawl out of your bucket if you don't have a lid?"

The fisherman replied, "No, don't worry. Because there are many crabs, I don't have to worry about any of them escaping."

"I don't understand; what do you mean by that?"

"You see, if I had one crab, it would climb out easily on its own. But because there are many crabs in the bucket, every time one crab tries to get out, another crab will grab it and pull it back down."

The same is true with our friends, family, and the people closest to us. Some people will grab us and pull us back down any time we try to succeed or do something different. It might seem odd. Your friends and family love you, so why would they want to hold you back? Well, remember the self-image I was talking about earlier? Your friends and family have self-images too.

For some, the minute they start to succeed or move to the next level, their self-image is threatened. Rather than trigger excitement, possible success triggers memories of past failures and the times they gave up.

"That's not true, Dan. If my friends and family were threatened by my success, then wouldn't they hate all successful people?"

It might be tempting to think that, but here's the thing. It's one thing when people see strangers succeed. It's completely different when they see someone they know—someone they grew up with—becoming successful. When they see a stranger succeed, they can say, "Yeah, they're successful, but they probably just got lucky." However, when

YOU succeed, your success is saying to them, "Hey, I came from the same place as you, and I made something of myself." They now have no excuses. When they don't have any excuses left, they'll criticize, judge, and mock you.

The way that they try to drag you down won't be apparent yet, but you'll hear it in phrases like:

- *"You used to be so good and polite ... what happened?"*
- *"I sacrificed so much for you; why are you doing this to me?"*
- *"Why are you trying to stand out?"*
- *"Why can't you be like them?"*
- *"Why don't you get a secure job first and then take risks?"*
- *"You're putting your family at risk!"*
- *"This isn't like you. You've changed."*

Have you heard any of those before?

Can you imagine what it's like to try to succeed when you're surrounded by judgment? It feels like climbing a mountain with a two-hundred-pound weight on your back. The saying "show me your friends and I'll show you your future" is true. We can't help but be affected by the people around us. It's very challenging to change your life without changing the people in it.

Think about it. If all your closest friends smoked, wouldn't it be hard for you not to smoke as well? Even if you don't smoke, you're exposed to secondhand smoke, which is even worse. On the other hand, what would happen if you spent most of your time around inspiring people like Jack Ma, Elon Musk, and Warren Buffett? Do you think your life would improve?

When people come to join my High-Ticket Closing® certification program, they come to learn a skill set. What they don't realize is that they are also joining a global community, a supportive community of like-minded people. Within hours of joining the program, they receive over one hundred comments of welcome and congratulations. Most people are shocked by how positive our community is. So after the program, you not only leave with a new skill but also with a group of people who will support you on your journey. It's a breath of fresh air for most people who are only used to people telling them they can't do something.

Can you imagine how much easier it would be if you had people cheering you on, no matter what you're going through? That's the power of changing your social circle. When you have positivity around you, you can't help but be positive as well. The great thing is, you can choose your friends. Choose to spend your time with people who add to your life, not people who take away from it.

CHAIN BREAKER:
YOU ARE WHO YOU HANG OUT WITH THE MOST.

INVISIBLE CHAIN #4: YOUR COMFORT ZONE

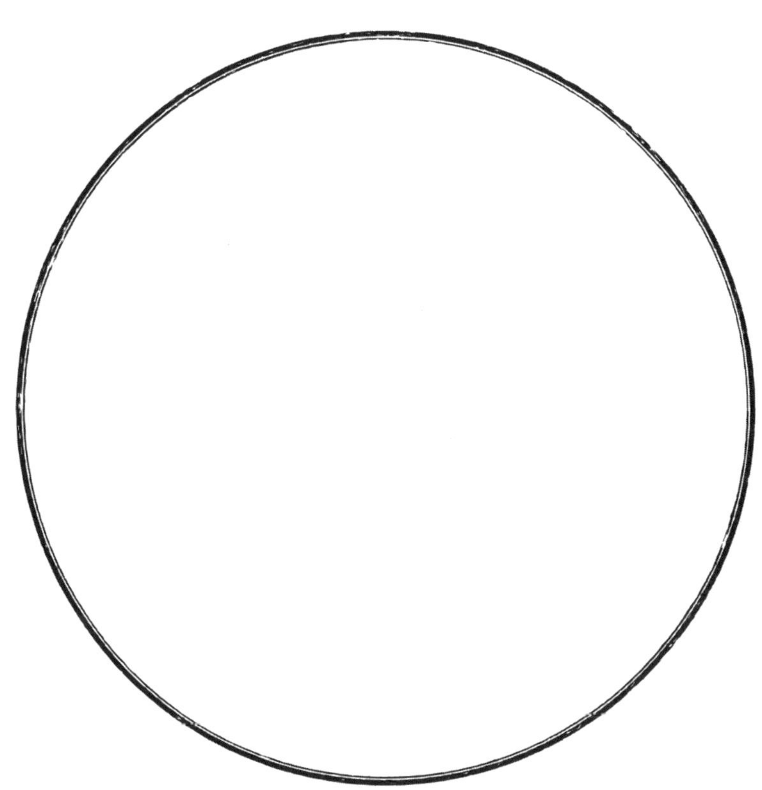

Let's do a powerful exercise together. This one exercise has transformed the way many of my students view success and comfort. You'll want to bring a pen out for this one. No, seriously—this is important. Grab a pen.

On the previous page, there is a circle. Inside that circle, write down everything you currently have or own, like your car, your home, your family, your friends, your job, your income, your spouse, your hobbies, etc. Take one to two minutes to do that right now. (You won't get the same effect if you don't write these down.)

Outside of the circle, list everything that you want but don't have, like your next home, your next car, that dream vacation, freedom, income, whatever it is that you want. Take another one to two minutes to do that as well. (Don't limit yourself here; write down everything you want.)

Now if you've followed along, you should have everything you currently have inside the circle. Everything you want but don't currently have is outside the circle. What's the point of all this? The things listed inside your circle represent your comfort zone. We are creatures of habit. We want to do the same things over and over again. If you look at what we do, it's quite repetitive from day to day. We eat the same things, go to the same places, hang out with the same people, work at the same job. We don't like to change. We want to operate with what we are comfortable with—this is our comfort zone.

Most people live inside their comfort zone their entire lives. That's why they don't change much year after year. However, here's the exciting thing—retake a look at the circle. Do you notice how everything you currently have is inside your comfort zone and how everything you want is outside your comfort zone? If you wanted something and you could get it, wouldn't you already have it? The reason you don't have something is that it's outside your comfort zone, and most people don't want to go outside their comfort zone. Everything you want but don't have is outside your comfort zone, including the income you want to have, the emotions you want to have, and the things you want to own.

MAGIC HAPPENS OUTSIDE YOUR COMFORT ZONE

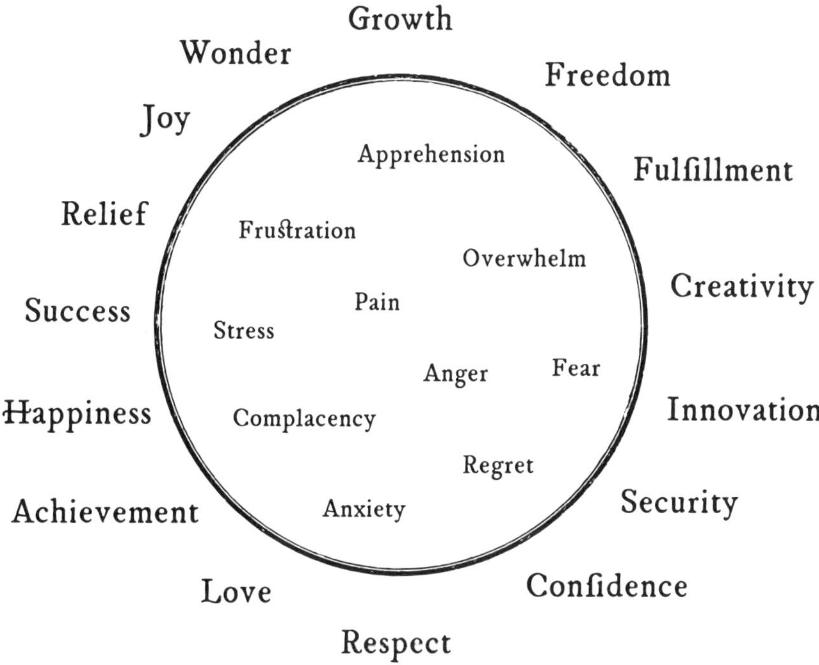

Once I went to go bungee jumping in Whistler (a town in the mountains outside of Vancouver). Here's something you should know about me—I don't like heights. Not surprisingly, as I walked up to the edge and saw the steep drop, my heart stopped. The employee helping me with the harness asked, "Are you ready to jump?"

"Uh ... y ... yeah. I guess so."

"Okay, then we'll count to three, and you'll jump. Sound good?"

"O ... okay."

"One ..." I felt my heart racing.

"Two ..." My legs froze up.

"Three!" I just stood there. Frozen in fear.

"Are you okay? Why didn't you jump?"

"Ye ... yeaah ... I'm fine. Let's try it again. But just let me count this time."

"All right. Whatever you say."

I took a few breaths and tried to psych myself up. "Okay, Dan. C'mon, you can do this—you're Dan Lok. A little bit of height shouldn't be enough to scare you. C'mon, you can do this."

I walked up to the edge once again and closed my eyes.

"One ..."

"Two ..."

"Three!"

I opened my eyes. I didn't jump. I was too scared. Now there was a line building up behind me, and people were putting on the pressure. "What's the holdup? If you can't jump, then just let us go ahead of you!"

The employee came up to me and said, "Hey, let's do it this way. Why don't you lean back over the edge and I'll hold onto the rope? We'll count to three, and I'll let go. That way you won't have to be the one that jumps. How does that sound?"

"Okay. That sounds good. Let's do it."

I walked up to the edge one more time. This time I was facing inward and leaned back over the edge. He held onto the rope as I was leaning back.

"One ..." I felt the fear rise up again.

"Two ..." I wanted to grab onto him for safety. But before I could ...

He let go.

"AHHHHHHH! AHHHHH!" I screamed as I fell toward the bottom.

"AHHHH!" I kept screaming as the bungee cord snapped me back up for a second drop.

"Ahh ..." I ran out of breath as I dangled at the bottom.

However, something happened after I jumped. You know what I'm talking about if you've ever gone bungee jumping. After the jump, I was THRILLED! I felt jolts of energy running through my body. I felt alive! I was excited and energized. After they pulled me up, I told them, "Let's do it again! That was awesome!"

That experience taught me that on the other side of fear is a feeling of joy. Pleasant emotions are outside your comfort zone, along with the other things you desire. Most people live inside their comfort zone and pay for it by feeling regret, fear, and overwhelm. People who live outside their comfort zone are rewarded with fulfillment, joy, and confidence.

YOUR COMFORT ZONE IS YOUR INCOME ZONE

Your comfort zone restricts more than just your emotions—it limits your income as well. If you aren't earning the income you would like to have, then most likely it's because you aren't willing to do what's uncomfortable for you. When you do what's uncomfortable, you'll be able to outearn the comfort seekers.

Below you'll see a list of comfortable versus uncomfortable actions. Can you see why those who perform uncomfortable actions have a higher potential?

COMFORTABLE	UNCOMFORTABLE
Let your boss determine your pay	Determine your own worth
Blame other people	Take responsibility for your own life
Point out problems	Provide solutions
Criticize others	Improve yourself
Be led by others	Lead others
Shoot down ideas	Turn ideas into reality
Blend in and be the same	Stand out and be different
Sacrifice long-term goals for short-term pleasure	Sacrifice short-term pleasure for long-term goals
Do what is easy	Do what is right
Move away from fear	Move towards fear

FEAR OF FAILURE VS. FEAR OF SUCCESS

You might think that most people don't act because they are afraid to fail, afraid to be criticized, or afraid to look bad in front of others, but what I've found is counterintuitive—fear of failure is not the main reason for people not taking action.

As H. P. Lovecraft wrote in his novel *Supernatural Horror in Literature*, "The oldest and strongest emotion of mankind is fear and the oldest and strongest kind of fear is fear of the unknown."

Most people don't act greater not because they fear failure, but because they fear success. They fear success because it is foreign to them. Success is unfamiliar territory, and it scares most people more than they realize. Success makes most people uncomfortable, and most people would rather stay comfortable than be happy. They say to themselves, "I know I'm not happy. I know where I want to be, but at least I'm comfortable—at least I know what to expect. Success is scary. I don't know what's going to happen if I succeed, and I'm not comfortable with that."

When you're afraid of success, it can show up in many ways. Some people choose to remain average. Some people sabotage their success. The latter is more confusing because on the surface it seems that you are doing everything you can, but you're subconsciously preventing yourself from reaching the next level. Here's an example.

I've seen many people go on what I call the "income roller coaster." You make money, and you lose it. You make money again, and you miss it, and you're not sure why. Somehow, some way, you lose any success that you're able to generate. It might've been a lousy partnership, a wrong decision, or just bad luck. If I were to sit down with you and ask, "What happened?" You'd reply, "Dan, I have no idea—it just somehow happened."

What they don't realize is that the ups and downs are a form of self-sabotage. The fear of success—the "emergency brake"—is on in your mind, so no matter how hard you push, your momentum stalls. So if you want to become comfortable with success, then learn to be comfortable being uncomfortable.

CHAIN BREAKER:
BE COMFORTABLE WITH BEING UNCOMFORTABLE.

INVISIBLE CHAIN #5: LOW EQ

I live in Vancouver, where it frequently rains during the winter months, which causes most people in the city to complain about the rain. They'll say, "It's too gloomy," or "I hate being wet," or "It's too cold."

However, when I drive with Jennie through the rain, guess what she says about the rain? She says, "I think the rain is romantic." You see, nothing has any meaning except the meaning you give it. Whether you feel joy, sorrow, frustration, overwhelm, bliss, anxiety, tranquility, or any other emotion, it's because YOU created that feeling. You attached meaning to an event, and then the related emotions followed.

Why else would some people feel one way about the rain, and Jennie would feel another way? It's the same rain—it's just that different meanings are attached to it.

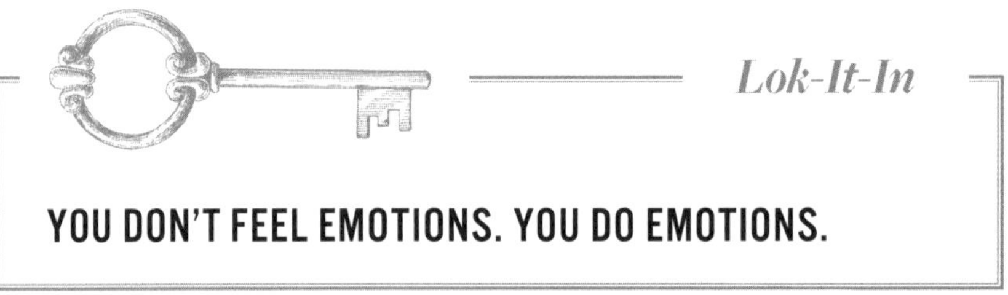

YOU DON'T FEEL EMOTIONS. YOU DO EMOTIONS.

When you are going through life, you'll realize that not many things are within your direct control. The weather, the traffic, the economy, the market circumstances, what people say about you, what people don't say about you, car accidents, health issues, gas prices, and so much more—none of these are within your direct control.

Most people will base their happiness and emotions on external events—events that they cannot control. If something good happens, they will be happy. If something terrible happens, they will be sad.

Can you see the problem with this? That's right—you have no control over your own emotions! If you have no control over your feelings, then you have no control over your mind. When you look at people who are struggling the most, you'll see they are emotionally affected by the smallest things:

- "Damn it—the train is late again."
- "God, would you look at the gas prices. They're up AGAIN."

- "You won't believe what she said to me at work today!"
- "There's nothing to watch on Netflix!"
- "Why is the internet so damn slow?"
- "I hate this. It's raining again."

However, if you look at the most successful people, you'll see they all remain calm and collected no matter what happens. They keep their emotions in check.

It is the unemotional, reserved, calm, detached warrior who wins, not the hothead seeking vengeance and not the ambitious seeker of fortune.

SUN TZU, *The Art of War*

For some reason, society wants you to think that you need a high IQ to be successful. They make you believe that you need to be book smart, have good grades, or have a degree to succeed. Here's the truth: you don't need any of that.

What you need is a high EQ—a high emotional quotient—the ability to control your emotions regardless of what happens. By having a high EQ, you'll bounce back quickly from mistakes, make better decisions under pressure, and become a better leader. When it comes to achieving success, EQ eats IQ for breakfast.

The great thing about EQ is that, unlike IQ, almost anyone can have a high EQ. You need to be aware it exists. EQ involves being more self-aware, having more empathy, understanding others, and knowing how to manage your own emotions. All of this is within your control. If you have a high EQ, you'll have a much higher chance of achieving your goals because you'll be undeterred by rejection, criticism, and failure.

**CHAIN BREAKER:
EQ EATS IQ FOR BREAKFAST.**

INVISIBLE CHAIN #6: TRYING TO SAVE EVERYONE

Who gets saved first during a coast guard helicopter rescue of capsized boat victims? What happens when there are more people in the water than space in the helicopter? Who do they save first? Their training instructs them to save the people who swim toward them first.

Why is that? Because they know if you try to save people who are flailing around in the water or swimming away from you first, you would be wasting your energy and risking more lives. It's the same when you are working toward success and significance—you cannot save everybody. You cannot help those who do not want help.

How many times have you done something for others, and they didn't even acknowledge your efforts? How many times has your help gone unappreciated? For me, that's happened too many times. When I first started being successful, my friends would ask me for help. They would invite me out to dinner and ask for advice.

However, after I gave them the advice, they would say, "Dan, that sounds great, but I think I'm going to do this instead." Then they would do it their way, fail, and then come back for advice again. Sometimes, it feels like you must help others because you have more than they do, but that's not true. You only have to help the people you want to help—you don't owe anything to anyone else.

Imagine you are on an airplane and a fire breaks out. The alarms start ringing. The cabin begins shaking, and the smoke starts rising.

The flight attendant goes on the speaker and yells, "Put on your oxygen mask first, before you assist others!" It's the old airplane analogy—secure your oxygen before helping others—otherwise, you'll do more harm than good. While it may seem noble to give up your own needs to help others, it doesn't work that way. You can't give away what you don't have. Instead, help yourself first. Take care of your own life, your income, your personal goals, and start thriving. Then you can give as much as you want because you'll have more than you need.

CHAIN BREAKER:
SAVE YOURSELF BEFORE YOU TRY TO SAVE THE WORLD.

INVISIBLE CHAIN #7: RELYING ON WILLPOWER

Have you ever seen those motivational videos on social media? You know, the ones where they tell you that as long as you have enough willpower, you'll succeed? Their theory is that if you push yourself hard enough and work yourself hard enough, you'll succeed no matter what your environment. I don't see it this way.

Have you ever woken up full of energy and motivation ready to start the day? You probably have. Have you also had days where you wake up and don't want to get out of bed? I'm pretty sure we've all had days like that. No matter how disciplined you are, willpower and motivation come and go.

People ask me, "Dan, how are you able to create so much impactful content across all social media platforms every single day? How are you so prolific when you still have a global organization to run? How do you manage all of the things you have going on?" The answer is simple. It's because I don't rely on willpower or motivation—I rely on structure.

Most people try to push toward their goals when they should take the opposite approach. Structure your time and environment so that you move toward your goal.

HOW TO STRUCTURE YOUR TIME FOR WORK-LIFE INTEGRATION

When you look at how most people structure their time, you'll see they try to achieve "work-life balance." The problem with that is it doesn't work when you're a high performer. Instead, if you want to perform at a high level, you want to achieve work-life integration, where the different pieces of your life all fit together perfectly so you don't have to use willpower or motivation to push toward your goals.

For example, when I travel for business, I also travel for leisure. When I go to a new city, I spend a few days developing business relationships, and then I book another couple of days to enjoy the area. That way I'm hitting multiple birds with one stone.

Here's another example. When I got involved in larger projects, it was getting more difficult to find time to practice martial arts, something that I love. So instead of relying on willpower and trying to squeeze in a couple of extra hours to practice, I integrated it into my life. A few of my team members wanted to learn martial arts, so I invited them to my house to practice. This way, even when I didn't want to practice on a particular day, my team would show up, and I'd have to practice with them whether I "felt like it" or not.

HOW TO STRUCTURE YOUR ENVIRONMENT FOR SUCCESS

If you were to enter my office today, you would see many "Wealth Triggers"—objects that remind me to think a certain way. On my desk, there is a clock to remind me of the value of time, a copy of Sun Tzu's *The Art of War* to remind me to think strategically, a small statue of a horse to trigger feelings of energy, and a picture of my mom and dad to remind me of my family values.

Even when I was still living in Surrey (the "hood" of Vancouver), I would do anything I could to upgrade my environment. I knew how powerful the situation could be. I would travel to downtown Vancouver and spend my day at Pan Pacific, one of the most expensive luxury hotels in the area. For that day, the upscale hotel would be my Wealth Trigger.

What Wealth Triggers can you put into your environment to remind you of the values you want to achieve? Changing my environment has worked for me; it has worked for my mentor and worked for my students who have put it into practice. Try it for yourself; see how you feel.

Most people rely on their willpower and motivation to succeed, and that is why they see inconsistent results. If you can structure your time and environment well, you'll feel the gravitational pull toward success without needing willpower at all.

CHAIN BREAKER:
RESULTS FOLLOW STRUCTURE, NOT WILLPOWER.

HOW MANY INVISIBLE CHAINS ARE HOLDING YOU DOWN?

Did you have any of these seven Invisible Chains? If you do, don't worry. Now that you know they exist, they are no longer invisible. Knowing these chains exist is half the battle. The other half is to take different actions once you see these chains pulling you down. Once you've broken the chains and released your "emergency brakes," it will be time to push down on the gas pedal.

CHAPTER 6

Unlock Your Productivity

IDEAL FOR: **CAGED LION, CHAINED MAGICIAN, INNOCENT PRISONER, HUSTLING TREASURE HUNTER, CASTAWAY**

Imagine you have a bank account that credits you with $86,400 every single day. You can use and spend this money however you like, but there is one catch—the balance doesn't carry over to the next day. Whatever you don't use or invest today will be gone tomorrow. There is no way to save it for another day. Knowing this, what would you do? You would use every dollar now, wouldn't you?

Well, you and I do have this bank account; it's called time. Every single day you have 86,400 seconds deposited to your life, your time bank. You can use each second however you like, but whatever you don't use or invest today is lost forever. Have you heard of the saying that "time is money"? Well, that's not true. Time is NEVER money. Time will always be more valuable than money because once the time is gone, it's gone forever. You can make more money, but you cannot make more time.

For you to unlock maximum productivity and success, here is one thing you must understand: time is your most valuable commodity. We all have the same amount of time to work with—the same 365 days in a year, the same seven days in a week, the same 86,400 seconds in a day. We all have the same time as Jeff Bezos, Bill Gates, Elon Musk, and Warren Buffett, but what separates them from everyone else is how they use their time.

The most successful and influential people today have mastered the art of maximum productivity, and in this chapter, you'll learn how to achieve maximum productivity as well. But before we can talk about productivity, we need first to define productivity.

It can be summed up in just five words. Productivity is the "maximum results in minimum time." That's it. Maximum results. In minimum time.

WHY I THINK THERE'S NO SUCH THING AS TIME MANAGEMENT

When you define productivity this way, you'll see that most conventional wisdom about productivity is completely off the mark. Most productivity advice talks about "time management," but when you think about it, can you manage time? Can you speed up time or make it slow down? Can you make time go backward? Can you deposit a few hours today and withdraw them tomorrow? Unless you're a genius like Tony Stark, the answer is no.

Since we all have the same 86,400 seconds in a day, the secret to productivity isn't time management—the secret to productivity is self-management. You can't manage time, but you can manage yourself. It's not about getting more hours into your day; it's about getting more results out of the hours you already have.

Over the years, I have read hundreds of books concerning the greats of the past and today's highly successful people. I have experimented and tested hundreds of different methods of productivity, time management, and high performance. All this was done to answer one question: "How can I get the most results in the least amount of time?"

I've boiled it down to five essential keys to unlocking maximum productivity. Some you may know; some you may not know. These are what have worked for me.

DAN'S FIVE KEYS TO UNLOCKING MAXIMUM PRODUCTIVITY

MAXIMUM PRODUCTIVITY KEY #1: BE ABSOLUTELY RUTHLESS ABOUT YOUR OUTCOME

Do you use "productivity" apps? Calendar apps, note-taking apps, to-do list apps, project management apps, and all the other apps. Do these apps make you more productive? These apps help you become efficient, but do they help you become productive?

Many people come up to me and say, "I'm doing the work, but for some reason, I do not see any results. What am I doing wrong?" I'd reply by asking them about what their day-to-day tasks are. They would then pull up their to-do list with dozens of items crossed off, then they'd say,

"You see, Dan? I'm doing so much every day, but I'm not getting any results. I'm not sure why."

"Okay, what kind of results are you looking for?"

"Well, I want to be more successful."

"Okay, and what does being more successful mean to you?"

"Oh, it means I want to generate more revenue. I want more clients."

"Okay—how much is that?"

"Well ... uh ... it would be ..."

I stop them right here. The uncertainty and lack of clarity about the potential outcome is the root of the problem. I provide clarity by asking a simple question, "Out of all these tasks you do every day, how many of these tasks are moving you toward the outcome you want?"

They would go through the list and realize most of what they do every day does not help their outcome. Most people are so concerned with moving quickly, getting more done, and staying busy that they forget to ask, "Is this even the direction I want to go?" Remember, the definition of productivity is maximum results in minimum time. Notice the emphasis on results. If you don't have a clear idea of your desired outcome, then how can you measure your results? It would be like playing basketball without a hoop; you can shoot all you want, but you would never score a single point.

Busyness is a form of laziness.

DAN LOK

WHAT DOES $10,000 A MONTH LOOK LIKE?

Imagine your goal is to make $10,000 a month. What can we do to become ruthless about our outcome? When the goal is too big or far away, action steps are less clear. That's why it's better to break down your goal into smaller actionable steps, so you know how to reach your outcome. For this example, let's break down the goal of $10,000 a month. First, let's see how much you would need to earn every week to hit $10,000 a month.

$10,000 / 4 weeks = $2,500 per week

And if you worked five days a week ...

$2,500 / 5 working days = $500 per day

What does this tell us? If you want to earn $10,000 a month, every day you need to hit $500. Can you see how this gives you more clarity? If you are not hitting your daily goal, then you are not hitting your weekly goal. If you are not hitting your weekly goal, then you are not hitting your $10,000 a month goal. Instead of waiting until the end of the month to find out, "Oops, I'm off track," you'll know every day whether you're heading toward your goal or not. That's what it means to be ruthless about your outcome.

WITH THE $500 PER DAY GOAL IN MIND, YOU CAN ASK YOURSELF QUESTIONS LIKE:

- Am I moving toward making $500 a day? Or away from it?
- How can I increase the value I'm delivering?
- What am I doing right now that I shouldn't be doing?
- What's the most efficient use of my time right now?
- What's the payoff of this activity I'm doing right now?

By asking yourself these questions, you'll move closer to your daily goal, then your weekly goal, and eventually your monthly goal.

WHAT DOES $1 MILLION A YEAR LOOK LIKE?

Let's say instead of making $10,000 a month, you want to aim higher. You want to earn $1 million a year. What would that look like to you? First, let's see how much you would need to earn in a month to make $1 million.

$1,000,000 / 12 months = $83,333.33 per month

Every month, you would need to earn $83,333 to get to a million dollars a year. That's still a lot of money—more than what most people make in a year. Let's break it down even further; let's see how much you would need to earn each week.

$83,333.33 / 4 weeks = $20,833.33 per week

Now let's see much you would need to earn every working day.

$20,833.33 / 5 working days = $4,166.67 per day

To earn $1,000,000 a year, you would need to make $4,166.67 every working day. Let's say you are working eight hours a day, then every hour of your day would be worth

$4,166.67 / 8 hours = $520.83 per hour

However, you and I both know that you can't be productive for the entire eight hours of a day; maybe one-third of your hours are genuinely productive. The rest of your time is spent taking breaks, checking emails, communicating, and other small tasks. To account for what a productive hour is worth for you, we would need to multiply the hourly rate by three.

$520.83 x 3 = $1,562.49 per hour

When you look at it this way, you'll see many of your daily activities aren't worth your time. You wouldn't be mowing your lawn, washing the dishes, doing paperwork, answering emails, or any "minimum wage activities." If you take two hours to mow your lawn, you didn't save money by not hiring someone else to do it. No. Those two hours just cost you about $3,000. If your goal is to make $1 million a year, then the question you should be asking yourself is, "Is what I'm doing right now worth $1,562.49 an hour?"

AVOID MINIMUM-WAGE ACTIVITIES.

Most people try to achieve their goals by working harder and longer. They'll take a second job, a night shift, a part-time gig. They try to add on more hours to hit their income goals. Adding on more hours isn't the answer. Adding more value is the answer. You can't double the hours in a day, but you can double the value you deliver.

When I first started, I could only charge $500 per project, which worked out to be less than minimum wage after all the hours worked. Every day, I would ask myself, "How can I increase the value I'm delivering? How can I charge more? How can I move closer to my daily income goal?" By asking myself those questions, I was able to charge more and more. Eventually, I charged more per hour than many people earned in a month. At one point, you would need to invest $10,000 an hour for my time as a consultant. (Now, these one-on-one consultations are no longer available. Why? The value I can create for the world with one hour of thinking and strategizing for my organization is more than the value I could create by consulting with another company.)

> ***Just because you are splashing around in the water, it doesn't mean you are swimming.***

How did I grow to that point? By being absolutely ruthless about my outcome every single day. That's the first key to maximum productivity. Just because you are splashing around in the water, it doesn't mean you are swimming.

EXERCISE: WHAT IS YOUR MAGIC NUMBER?

WHAT IS YOUR MAGIC NUMBER?

Your magic number is the number you'll need to earn every single day if you want to hit your goal. By being clear on what this number is, you'll know whether you are on-track or off-track. The more clarity you have, the more power you have.

- How much do you want to earn per year? ________
- Divide the top number by 12 to get your monthy income. ________
- And now divide that number by 4 to get your weekly income. ________
- Divide that number by 5 to get your daily income. ________
- Divide it once more by 8 to get your hourly rate. ________
- And finally, multiply that number by 3 to get your productive hour rate - your magic number. ________

WHAT IS YOUR MAGIC NUMBER?

____

MAXIMUM PRODUCTIVITY KEY #2: STAY LASER-BEAM FOCUSED

Have you noticed that it's becoming harder than ever to stay focused? Daily your phone is bombarded with notifications, people are constantly emailing you, new movies are coming out, new shows are coming out, and new products are being released. The world is becoming noisier than ever.

When was the last time you focused on one task for at least two hours without checking your phone or email? If you're like most people, then you probably have trouble staying focused on one task for long periods of time. The funny thing is, although I have a global following on social media, I personally don't spend too much time on social media. When I'm working, I block out time to work. I unplug my phone, turn off all notifications, and I don't check any emails. When I work, I just work. It's not just about how many hours you can put into doing important work; it's about doing very focused work.

Distraction is only the luxury for average people. Laser-beam focus is mandatory for success.

DAN LOK

SNIPER APPROACH VS. SHOTGUN APPROACH: HOW TO GET MORE RESULTS BY GETTING LESS DONE

Being busy has become a badge of honor for some people. It's ridiculous. These people are constantly checking their phones, answering emails, and stepping out for "important phone calls." They're never present in the moment. These people are operating by what I call the "shotgun approach." They spray and pray. They do many things at once and hope one of the bullets lands. They're frantic, scattered, uncoordinated. They live life at one hundred miles per hour.

I prefer the "sniper approach." When you think of a sniper, what comes to mind? They're cool, calm, and collected. They scout out their position, locate their target, and pull the trigger—one shot, one kill. The sniper believes that less is more. They believe in precision over power, focus over distraction, and humility over ego. Snipers understand that not all actions lead to results. They know that many actions are wasteful and counterproductive.

THE 80/20 PRINCIPLE

The 80/20 Principle states that approximately 80 percent of all effects come from 20 percent of the causes. To put it more accurately, the *majority of effects come from a minority of the causes.*

- The majority of sales in a company come from a minority of their products.[2]
- A minority of the teams dominates most sports. The Lakers and Celtics account for close to half of the NBA championships (thirty-three out of seventy), and just five of the thirty NBA teams account for 69 percent of the titles.[3]
- According to Dr. Gabriel Zucman from the University of California at Berkeley, the top 0.1 percent of the American population owns more of the American wealth than the bottom 80 percent of the American population.[4]

---

2 Richard Koch, The 80/20 Principle: The Secret to Achieving More with Less (London: Nicholas Brealey Publishing01).

3 NBA Advanced Stats, NBA, accessed August 1319, https://stats.nba.com/.

4 Gabriel Zucman, World Inequality Database, accessed August 1319, https://wid.world/.

It doesn't just stop there though—in your own life, 20 percent of your actions will account for 80 percent of your happiness, income, and success.

What does this have to do with you? Well, when you find out which 20 percent of your actions create the most results for you, you can eliminate the other 80 percent. Instead of a "to-do list," you can create a "not to-do list" and increase your focus.

80/20 PRINCIPLE EXERCISE

You can see how the 80/20 Principle is impacting your life with a simple exercise. Think back to last week and everything you've done, and now fill out the exercise below:

1. **"WHAT IS STRESSING ME OUT?"** - List out the main activities that have been causing you stress.
2. **"WHAT HAS BEEN SUCCESSFUL?"** - List out what has produced the most results for you in the last week.
3. **"ADD THE NOT-TO-DO LIST"** - What are some of the stressful activities that you could delegate or eliminate completely?
4. **"ADD THE TO-DO LIST"** - What are some of the successful actions you could repeat next week?

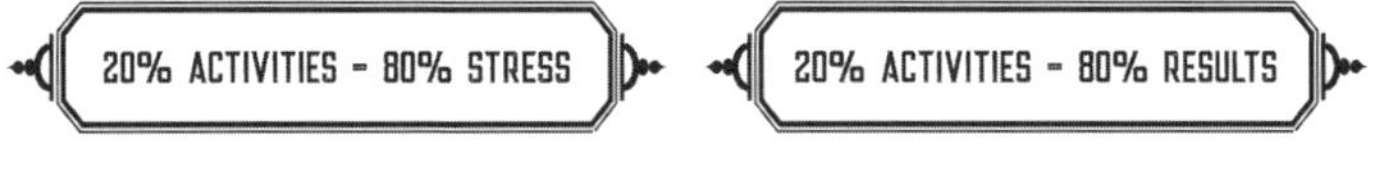

WHAT IS STRESSING ME OUT?

-
-
-
-

ADD TO NOT TO-DO LIST:

-
-

WHAT HAS BEEN SUCCESSFUL?

ADD TO-DO LIST:

FOCUS ON THE FEW, NOT THE MANY

Remember, being productive isn't about adding on more work; it's about taking away what is unnecessary and focusing on the few critical drivers for maximum results. It's not about fitting as many actions as you can into your day; it's about focusing on the few actions that make all the difference. Know what needs to be done and eliminate everything else.

MAXIMUM PRODUCTIVITY KEY #3: STRUCTURE YOUR TIME LIKE A BILLIONAIRE

Have you ever wondered how billionaires like Bill Gates structure their time? After all, they have the same amount of time we do, but for some reason, they get so much more done—why is that?

Well, one reason is because of Parkinson's law. It says that "work expands to fill the time available for its completion." Now what does that mean?

Have you ever had a deadline that was months ahead and yet didn't pay any attention to the task until the due date was fast approaching? That's Parkinson's law in action: work takes up the amount of time available for doing the job.

Bill Gates schedules his appointments in six-minute increments. I have mine in fifteen-minute increments. I set aside blocks of time for everything I do during the day. This control gives me the freedom to do what I love to do every day.

PROCRASTINATION EQUALS POVERTY.

SCRIPT YOUR DAY; DON'T SCHEDULE

If you want to have productive days, script your day out; don't schedule it. What is the difference between scripting and scheduling? Scheduling is based on what other people want from you. Scripting is intentionally blocking out time for your goals and outcomes.

After you have a clear outcome and know the actions to take to achieve this goal, what's next? You have to set a time to get it done! You probably know this already, but nothing gets done without a deadline.

Do you know the single word that kills most dreams? "Someday."

"Someday, I'll travel the world."

"Someday, I'll take my wife and kids to Disney World."

"Someday, I will pay off my debt."

"Someday, I will quit my job."

"Someday, I'll write my book."

That deadly word: "someday."

It's always "someday," but take a look at the calendar. There is Monday, Tuesday, Wednesday, Thursday, Friday, Saturday, Sunday. Where is "someday"? It doesn't exist. It is an illusion made up so people don't feel bad about procrastinating. Imagine a business owner who says, "Someday, I will get that customer. Someday, I will close that sale, and someday I'll scale my business." How much money will a business owner like this make? Zero.

Unsuccessful people use "someday"; successful people use "today."

"Today, I'm going to take action."

"Today, I'm going to close that sale."

"Today, I'm going to attract more customers."

"Today, I am going to make it happen."

When you use "someday," you are putting off your dreams, your goals. You think that you will do it when you are ready. However, someday never comes, and you'll never be "ready." Successful people understand that you don't have to get it right; you have to get it going. Script your day today. If it's not scripted, it won't happen.

MAXIMUM PRODUCTIVITY KEY #4: ELIMINATE THE SEVEN INNER DEMONS OF PROCRASTINATION

We all procrastinate from time to time. There are Seven Inner Demons of Procrastination you need to know. If you can recognize the Seven Inner Demons as they appear, you'll be able to eliminate them much more easily.

HOW TO ELIMINATE THE SEVEN INNER DEMONS OF PROCRASTINATION

Pretend that you are about to do a simple push-up. The Seven Inner Demons of Procrastination then enter your mind. How many do you recognize?

1. THE PERFECTIONIST

"Let me make sure the spacing between my hands is correct first. Also, I've got to have the perfect angle at the elbows. I shouldn't get too close to the floor; if I hit the floor that would be cheating—it wouldn't be a proper push-up. You know what, I'm not even wearing the proper athletic gear; let me change, and then I'll do the push-up."

The Perfectionist is so concerned with doing the perfect push-up that they don't even get started doing one. Who do you think will be further ahead? The person who waits a month and then does one perfect push-up, or the person who does ten imperfect push-ups every day for a month? Of course, it's the person who DOES the push-ups. The Perfectionist is too concerned with perfection, when all you need is progress.

Remember—you don't have to get it perfect; you have to get it going.

2. THE LAZY SLACKER

"I don't want to do it—it looks hard. Is there an easier version? Maybe there's a push-up machine that can do it for me?"

The Lazy Slacker hates doing work. They hate anything that makes them slightly uncomfortable. They want the results, but not the work it takes to get there. What they don't realize is that anything worth achieving will take hard work.

3. THE MEASURER

"I can only do ten push-ups right now but look at him—he can do twenty. And look at her; she can do thirty. I'm no good; I suck. I should stop doing push-ups."

Measurers compare themselves to everyone else. If there is someone out there doing it better, they will get discouraged. Even when they know they are just a beginner, they won't do something unless it feels better. Who cares? It's not about them; it's about the progress you are making toward your goal. There will always be someone better than you. If you let that fact stop you from acting, then you'll be stuck for a very long time.

4. THE FUTURIST

"If I do a push-up, then wouldn't I have a really big triceps? What if I want a large biceps? Wouldn't it look weird if my triceps were big and my biceps were small? What if I wanted to build out my shoulder? Am I going to look like one of those really weird, big, bulky guys? I don't want that; then no one is going to want to date me. Let's not do any push-ups; I don't want that."

The Futurist thinks so far ahead into the future and creates problems that don't even exist! If you're a Futurist, you overthink everything and make things a bigger deal than they are. It's just a push-up; no need to think so far into the future. It's the same when people come up and ask me, "Dan, what should I invest in?" But later, I discover that they still haven't paid off their debt. Take it one step at a time—don't think too far into the future and create imaginary problems.

5. THE IDIOT

"I don't know how to do a push-up. Do you have any books or videos on how to do a push-up?"

The Idiot overcomplicates the simplest tasks. It's just a push-up. You go down, and then you push yourself up. It's not complicated, but the Idiot needs to read five hundred books on push-ups and watch two hundred training videos on the advanced types of push-ups before acting. Meanwhile, someone else is doing twenty push-ups every day and building that foundational strength. Can you do any of the advanced push-ups if you can't even do ten regular push-ups? You can't, so why waste your time pretending you don't know how to do a push-up? Just do the push-up.

6. THE DUMB LISTENER

Listener: "All right, I'm going to do a push-up now."

Friend: "Why are you doing push-ups? Science says it's bad for you. Do cardio instead."

Listener: "Oh? Okay, let me try cardio."

Listener: "Cardio isn't working; I'm still weak."

Friend #2: "Don't do cardio; cardio doesn't work anymore. Here, try this pill. It works way better than cardio and push-ups."

The Dumb Listener has the "shiny object syndrome," falling for whatever sounds good. Instead of just doing the push-ups and committing to improving their push-ups, they will listen to what other people sell them on. They will change their minds multiple times and never focus. They can't commit to one thing and continually look for others to give them direction. What they don't understand is that wealth is acquired by committing to one idea over time.

WEALTH IS COMMITTING TO ONE IDEA OVER TIME.

7. THE EXCUSE MAKER

"I can't do a push-up; the floor is dirty. There are germs and bacteria on the floor; I'm going to get sick. And what if my bones aren't strong enough for a push-up? I don't want to break my arm. I'll not do the push-up."

The Excuse Maker makes up all the excuses you can think of to not do the push-up. The excuses are mostly irrational, but they are enough to stop them from doing what they know they should do.

What should you do when you see the Seven Inner Demons of Procrastination show up?

ACTION DRIVES OUT THOUGHT

THOUGHT --> **ACTION**

(When the gap is too long, procrastination wins.)

THOUGHT --> **ACTION**

(Beat procrastination by shortening the gap from thought to action.)

Think of these demons as rabid wolves waiting to feed. If you feed them, they will continue to grow and growl louder. However, if you resist the temptation to feed them, they will weaken. Whenever you recognize that one of the seven has shown up, here's what you do: take action, because action drives out thought.

Have you ever experienced procrastination once you've already started something? Probably not, because procrastination shows up strongest before you take action. Develop the habit of shortening the gap between thought and action. The longer the gap between thought and action, the stronger the procrastination becomes. The less time it takes for you to start, the weaker the procrastination becomes.

MAXIMUM PRODUCTIVITY KEY #5: DEVELOP YOUR NONNEGOTIABLES

Your nonnegotiables are actions you take every day no matter what. These are the things that keep every part of your life strong and thriving. If you stop exercising or doing any physical activity for a long time, you become weak and fragile. This same idea applies to every other part of your life. If you don't take the time to maintain it, it will weaken.

Your nonnegotiables should align with the outcomes you want to achieve. Because of this, it is necessary for you to have a clear understanding of your goal and to keep focused on what you wish to achieve. I have specific nonnegotiables that help me move toward my goals. You might have different ones.

DAN LOK'S NONNEGOTIABLES

BUSINESS WELL-BEING: Sixty minutes a day spent on thinking, developing strategies, and keeping a pulse on my team.

EMOTIONAL WELL-BEING: Thirty minutes a day spent on a morning ritual that includes visualization, Attitude of Gratitude meditation, and deep breathing exercises.

FINANCIAL WELL-BEING: Thirty minutes a day looking at financials and investments and reviewing numbers.

GROWTH: Sixty minutes a day learning. This includes reading, consulting with experts, and meeting with other founders and CEOs.

PHYSICAL WELL-BEING: Sixty minutes a day of physical exercise, three times a week.

FINANCIAL MASTERY IS SELF-MASTERY

These are the five keys that have unlocked my productivity over the years. Before financial mastery, you must have self-mastery, because if you can't control yourself, then how can you expect to control money?

Now that you are aware of the five keys, it's your turn to implement them and act—don't procrastinate. Be ruthless about your outcome, stay laser-beam focused, structure your day like you're a billionaire, eliminate your inner demons, and remain committed to your nonnegotiables. If you can do that, you'll be shocked at how much you can accomplish.

CHAPTER 7

Unlock Your Sales

IDEAL FOR: **ALL WEALTH ARCHETYPES**

Recently, I gave a talk at an invite-only meeting for a group of highly successful entrepreneurs, all leading companies and organizations with $1 million to $100 million in revenue. These were steely, skeptical people who had seen and heard it all before. However, by the end of the talk, every person in the audience was furiously taking down notes and asking questions. They had so many questions that I couldn't get out of the room for an hour until all their questions got answered.

What was the topic that got all of these entrepreneurs and founders so riled up? I was talking about the new age of advanced selling, what I call High-Ticket Closing®. The "good old days" of selling through cold calling are long gone. People are smarter and more skeptical than ever. As soon as they hear, "Hello, how are you?" they know it's a cold call and hang up immediately. Customers can quickly sign up for "Do Not Call" lists, block phone numbers, and ignore any attempts at unsolicited phone calls. The sales environment has become challenging.

Think about it—even when you think of the word "sales," you immediately think about a slimy, "snake oil" salesperson who tries to manipulate you into doing something you don't want to do. I'm not saying that the telephone is no longer an excellent way to generate sales. The phone is a superb Conversion tool. However, the phone is a horrible lead generation tool.

You don't have to agree, but I believe that how a customer buys is more important than what a customer buys. The customer's frame of mind is crucial to the sale and the ongoing relationship with the customer. Imagine you are walking in a shopping mall and you see a booth giving out free samples. The people working at the booth ask you to try a free sample. They interrupt your day. How do you respond to this? You walk around them, you avoid them, or you ignore them because they are an unwanted interruption.

What they don't realize is that people love to buy, but they hate to be sold. You don't want to be sold, nor do I. We want to believe that we are in charge of our own buying decisions. Even if we do buy from a pushy salesperson, we somehow feel like they "got us" and we don't feel good about the sale. That's why cold calling does not work anymore. When you are cold calling someone with whom you have no prior relationship, with no value added first, with no positioning, it's a very steep uphill climb. When you are cold calling, the problem is you are trying to build all that trust and credibility in a short amount of time, and no matter how good you are at sales, you are putting yourself at a severe disadvantage.

People love to buy, but they hate to be sold.

DAN LOK

So, what do you do if cold calling doesn't work for lead generation? You let marketing take care of that. I rely on my marketing, branding, and social media to generate leads. I make those who are interested come to me by booking a call through one of my closers. It creates a better experience for the closer and the prospect. It's the difference between having someone raise their hand and say, "I'm interested in this!" versus physically pulling and forcing someone to raise their hand when they don't even want to move.

When they book a call with one of my closers, I have their full attention. When you are cold calling someone, you have no idea what they are doing or if you're interrupting their day. However, when they book a time with you, you will have their full attention for that time. When you call them, you are a salesperson. When they call you, you are the expert.

That's why I've created a new way, a new methodology of closing to meet the changing times. I call it High-Ticket Closing®. It's a form of closing by focusing on selling premium products and services in which closers only take inbound calls generated from marketing. Take these rules. Implement them. You'll be astounded at the results.

THE FIVE RULES OF HIGH-TICKET CLOSING®

Remember, we're not talking about cold calling, door knocking, or any of the greasy, sleazy sales techniques. In those cases, you are acting like an annoying pest. However, with High-Ticket Closing®, you are a welcome guest. You are not interrupting someone's day by calling unexpectedly or knocking on their door in the middle of dinner—that's not the purpose of High-Ticket Closing®. We are not talking about becoming a sleazy salesperson. We are talking about being a professional. We're not pushing or manipulating people—we are helping them come to their own decision.

Imagine a prospect is looking to buy, but they still have doubts. They need some more information, more guidance, more clarity on how the process will work. After all, it's not a small purchase. Wouldn't it make sense if someone spoke with them on the phone to walk them through the process and answer any questions they may have? High-Ticket Closing® is about making a one-on-one human connection. Think about the people in your life whom you care about the most—your parents, your siblings, your friends. When they are going through tough times and you want to help, how do you do it? You don't do it through a social media post, a website, or anything online. You help them through the telephone or face to face. In those intimate moments, you need that human connection. That is what High-Ticket Closing® is all about.

Now, you may still have some questions about the differences between High-Ticket Closing® and traditional sales. So why don't I show you exactly what I mean by High-Ticket Closing®?

HIGH-TICKET CLOSING® RULE #1: DON'T SOUND LIKE A SALESPERSON

Now, without thinking—very quickly, tell me when you hear the word "sales," what pops into your mind? If you're like most people, you'll probably think, "Oh, it's a used car salesperson," or "snake-oil," or "liars," or "scam artist." Whatever it is, much negativity comes to mind.

Now, when I say the word "salesperson," what comes to mind? What's the image that you have? Maybe you've seen certain movies, where it makes you think, "Oh, those are the salespeople; they're going to try to sell me," or "They are going to lie to me," or "They are just going after my money." Whatever image you have in your mind, it's most likely a negative image—that's the image society has of salespeople.

Whenever you sound, talk, or act like a typical salesperson, it creates resistance. That's why you never, ever, ever want to sound like a typical salesperson; it immediately turns off the prospect.

Picture a salesperson and how they talk. What do they sound like to you? How do they act? How do they communicate? What comes to mind? You might picture a salesperson talking quickly, with a lot of enthusiasm, and they are trying to project a lot of energy. They push features and benefits on you without listening, without slowing down, without actually understanding your problems. That's what a typical salesperson sounds like most of the time.

You want to do the exact opposite. Typical salespeople talk fast, while High-Ticket Closers® slow down. Salespeople push features and benefits, while High-Ticket Closers® listen intently. Salespeople jump around with enthusiasm, while High-Ticket Closers® stay calm and collected as a professional.

HIGH-TICKET CLOSING® RULE #2: THE LESS YOU TALK, THE MORE YOU CLOSE

The most common mistake that salespeople make is talking too much. Sometimes the person talks so much that they talk the prospect out of the sale. Has this ever happened to you? You've made up your mind to buy, but the salesperson keeps on talking and talking. Then you get annoyed, and you say to the salesperson, "You know what; I'm busy right now. I've got to go. I'll come back later."

This rebuttal is very, very common. You see, one of the myths (believed by many people) is that a great salesperson is always talking, always pushing, always shoving the product or service, and they're still trying to change how people feel about a particular topic. However, that's not what we do with High-Ticket Closing®.

High-Ticket Closing® is all about asking the right questions at the right time with finesse.

There are many different types of questions to ask: open-ended questions, close-ended questions, discovery questions, and redirection questions. There are so many great questions to ask! In just a few pages, you'll learn which type of questions to ask, how to ask them, and when to ask them.

Why do you think this is important? It's because when you are talking, you are not listening, and when you are not listening, you aren't learning about your prospect. If you don't know anything about your prospect, then you can't help them solve their problems. I firmly believe that when you say something, it means something. When the prospect says something, it means everything. You could tell them what they need to hear; it's much more powerful to step back and ask the proper questions. You ask the right questions, extract the correct information, and you let the prospect say it instead of you saying it.

Have you ever read a sales book that was going to teach you "101 ways to close a prospect" or "59 ways to handle this one objection"? I don't believe in that approach, and I don't teach my students this either. Why? It's tough to connect with someone when your head fills with thoughts about exactly what you're going to say next. At that point, you're not having a conversation. You're just waiting for your turn to talk.

I prefer to keep it very simple. My closing line is usually, "Hey, what would you like to do?" or "Where should we go from here?" That's it. If I have done my job during the entire call, if I have asked the right questions and discovered the prospect's pain, then saying "yes" to the sale becomes a natural, logical conclusion. I don't need to twist the arms and say, "HEY! Do you want to buy right now?" or the good ol' alternative close, "Would you like it in blue or red?" In High-Ticket Closing®, we don't do any of that, nor do we want to.

Remember—High-Ticket Closing® is about asking the right questions at the right time with finesse.

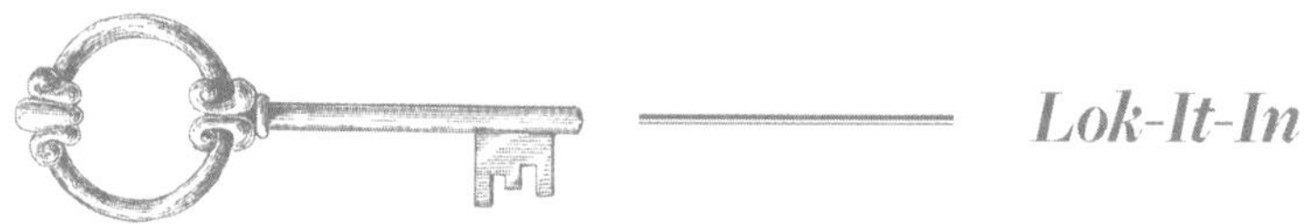

Lok-It-In

**WHEN YOU SAY SOMETHING, IT MEANS SOMETHING.
WHEN THE PROSPECT SAYS SOMETHING,
IT MEANS EVERYTHING.**

HIGH-TICKET CLOSING® RULE #3: PEOPLE DON'T BUY THEIR WAY INTO SOMETHING; THEY BUY THEIR WAY OUT OF SOMETHING

People buy to get out of their pain, to escape from a particular situation. They want to lose weight and escape the shame of being overweight. They want to get rid of their debt and stop feeling constant financial stress. They want to take that vacation and escape the monotony of their jobs.

When there is no pain, there is no sale. When the prospect does not have a problem, they have no reason to buy. Sometimes, people will have a problem but won't admit it to themselves. That's why it's the job of the High-Ticket Closer® to make it crystal clear to the prospect of how investing in the product or service today will help them change their lives and escape their pain. When you think of it this way, can you see why the standard salesperson's "show and tell" doesn't work? They get all enthusiastic and energetic, put on a fake smile, and "shotgun" all the features and benefits into the prospect's face, hoping something will hit.

What the salesperson fails to realize is that people don't buy because they understand the product; people buy because they feel understood. That's why when the prospect brings up objections most salespeople are stuck on the defensive trying to justify the value of the offer. Instead, a High-Ticket Closer® always has the prospect's best interest at heart. They ask, "What is the pain they are trying to escape?" or "How can I help them?" or "Would they be a good fit for this offer, or should I send them away?"

Now, this might not always be a pleasant experience for the prospect—after all, you are digging into their deepest pains. However, solving the prospect's problem is like cleansing a wound—sometimes, it stings a bit in the beginning before it starts to get better. Think about a doctor. Do you think a doctor would be effective if they weren't willing to make their patient a bit uncomfortable? Imagine a doctor who won't give you a flu shot because they're scared it might hurt you for a second—that wouldn't be a very good doctor now, would it?

THE THREE MAGIC WORDS

Have you ever seen the antismoking ad that compared a regular person's lung to a smoker's lung? One was healthy and had a vibrant pink color; the other was gray, shriveled, and unhealthy. By painting a clear vision of what happens when you smoke, that ad made an emotional impact on many people. In High-Ticket Closing®, it's a very similar thing. You want to reveal the gap between where the prospect is and where the prospect wants to go. We accomplish this through three magic words: Exactly, Specifically, and Precisely.

Instead of asking, "What kind of results are you looking for?" you ask, "EXACTLY what kind of results are you looking for?"

Instead of asking, "What have you done in the past to try to generate more sales?" you ask, "What SPECIFICALLY have you done in the past to try to generate more sales?"

Instead of asking, "What were you hoping to get from me today?" you ask, "PRECISELY what were you hoping to get from me today?"

By asking these questions using these specific words, you are guiding your prospect into being detailed in their answers, which helps you to discover more and more about them: their pains, their goals, and what EXACTLY, SPECIFICALLY, and PRECISELY they are looking to get.

You will find with experience that these three words will become part of your everyday script, and you will be able to use them in your day-to-day life as well. People love being asked about themselves and will go into detail if you give them a chance; it makes them feel cared for and important.

HIGH-TICKET CLOSING® RULE #4: ALWAYS FIND THEIR LEVEL 3 PAIN

There are three levels of pain that you can discover on a closing call:

- **LEVEL 1 PAIN**: Surface-level pain (intellectual problem, can easily be identified)
- **LEVEL 2 PAIN**: Business or financial pain
- **LEVEL 3 PAIN**: Personal pain

Why are these levels so important? Because when there is no pain, there is no sale. As harsh as it sounds, it's the job of the High-Ticket Closer® to help the prospect realize the consequences of not making a change in their lives.

When we are talking about Level 1 Pain, we are talking about the problem the prospect arrives with in the beginning. When the prospect explains their problem, they are very intellectual about it and emotionally uninvested. However, we all know that there are always more deep-seated reasons for someone to come to you. The prospect might go to you and say, "I'm here because I want more customers for my business." If you dig deep, you'll find there is another level of pain for them—Level 2 Pain: business or financial pain.

Let's say you then ask the prospect, "Well, how many customers are you getting currently? It can't be that bad; can it?" In answering this question, they will talk about their problem and reveal to you something more in depth. You may discover that they are currently losing money because it's a slow season for them. You've just dug deeper and revealed a deeper level of pain. However, there is one level deeper—Level 3 Pain: personal pain. What would this look like to you?

Well, you might ask the prospect a few more questions and discover that their business is a family-owned business passed down from generation to generation. If they don't get more customers, their family business could shut down. Now that is Level 3 Pain. When you are digging for Level 3 Pain, what you discover may not always be this extreme but just trying to get to Level 3 Pain would be more effective than trying to address Level 1 Pain. When there is no pain, there is no emotional investment. When there is no emotional investment, there is no sale.

You might be thinking, "Okay, Dan, that makes sense. But how do I get to that Level 3 Pain?" You use discovery questions—questions designed to get more information about your prospect. Here are some discovery questions you can use to help dig deeper into the prospect's pain:

- "Tell me more about that."
- "Can you be more specific? What's one example?"
- "How long has that been a problem?"
- "What have you tried to do about that? And did that work?"
- "How much do you think that has cost you?"
- "How do you feel about that?"
- "How have you tried to deal with the problem?"

When you get to Level 3 Pain and get to the core of the problem, you'll gain more trust from the prospect, more credibility, and you'll find it becomes easy to close any prospect, no matter how large the deal is.

HIGH-TICKET CLOSING® RULE #5: DON'T CLOSE BAD POTENTIAL CUSTOMERS

If you've ever dealt with a bad client, you know how tiring and stressful it can be. Whether they are a client who is always complaining, too demanding, or just plain difficult, you don't want to close bad potential clients or customers. It does no good for either you or the business. Remember, this is a process where YOU are evaluating the prospects as much as they are deciding on you. You want to retain the customers you gain, and bad customers leave a sour taste in everyone's mouth.

Don't save people who don't want saving. Imagine running in a race where you have to drag the runner from start to finish—it's not going to be fun. If they're not willing to run on their own two legs, they likely won't do well with your offer either. If you are selling programs, this means that they must want to implement what they learn. If you are selling products, this means they need to use the product. If you are a consultant, it means you need to pick clients who will execute your advice.

How do you reject bad customers or clients? You tell them it's not a good fit. There will be other customers and clients who will be a great fit—that's the beauty of choice. When you are a High-Ticket Closer®, you live in abundance, and you don't have to do things that go against your moral compass or values.

Don't take on clients who:

- Are negative
- Bring drama into your world
- Always come to you with never-ending problems
- Always ask for your time and ask you to open up your schedule no matter what hour of the day
- Make unreasonable demands or have unreasonable expectations

Life is too short, and as you already know, time is our most valuable commodity. No need to waste it on people who don't want our help or people who don't appreciate our help. How much better would your life be if you never had to deal with negative people again? You have a choice, and you deserve to choose who you have as a customer or client.

THE HIGH-TICKET CLOSING® METHODOLOGY

HOW TO NATURALLY AND LOGICALLY MOVE THE PROSPECT TO THEIR OWN DECISION

Now that you understand the psychology and rules of High-Ticket Closing®, it's time to get into the details of the High-Ticket Closing® call. These calls are conducted with class, calmness, and confidence (you'll see why in just a second). Once you understand the stages of a call and how to run the call, you'll be able to close deals with much more ease, especially with the more sophisticated and affluent customers.

THE THREE STAGES OF A HIGH-TICKET CLOSING® CALL

There are three stages of every call. As you go through each step, you move closer toward your goal of closing the sale. These steps are like a staircase for you to steadily proceed toward the close. They're meant to go in order, so no steps should be skipped or eliminated.

It's designed to keep you, the High-Ticket Closer®, in complete control of the call from beginning to end. It's a logical progression from introduction to close that makes the call effortless. You'll see that these stages don't rely on enthusiasm, gimmicks, or memorizing scripts. It's a combination of the science of human behavior and your finesse. Once you fully internalize this script, you'll be able to connect deeply with your prospect.

STAGE ONE: THE AGENDA

Stage one is where the call begins, and you set the frame for the call. The prospect will make a judgment about you within the first few seconds of hearing you speak, so this is vital.

In this stage, you are setting the tone for the way business will be conducted; you'll get some basic commitments, understand their motivation, and discover the needs of the prospect.

This stage should take no longer than five minutes to finish.

HIGH-TICKET CLOSER® EXAMPLE:

Prospect: "Hello, is this Dan?"

Closer: "Yes, this is Dan. What can I do for you?"

Prospect: "Oh, I'm calling in for the appointment we had scheduled."

Closer: "Yes, for 3:00 p.m. So, Mrs. Prospect, why did you want to book the call with me today?"

Prospect: "Well, I'm looking for X, Y, and Z."

Closer: "That's great. Now, I need to ask some questions about your business to see if we are a good fit and how we can add value to what you're doing. How does that sound?"

With just a few sentences, you've established credibility, gained a small commitment, and set the expectations for the call with your prospect as opposed to the typical salesperson.

TYPICAL SALESPERSON EXAMPLE:

Salesperson: "Hi, Mr. Prospect. How are you doing today?"

Prospect: "Doing well."

Salesperson: "Great, and if I could have a minute of your time today, I think you'll love some of the offers we have for a limited time right now. Is this a bad time to talk?"

Don't you hate those calls?

After you've set the stage and expectations for the prospect, the next step is to qualify the prospect to make sure they are a good fit.

STAGE TWO: THE QUALIFYING

Remember that when there is no pain, there is no sale. Stage Two is where we discover everything about the prospect's pain, needs, wants, and everything else. By the end of this stage, you should know:

- What are their needs, wants, and desires?
- Who are they doing this for?
- Where do they want to be?

- Why are they considering your offer right NOW and not later?
- Can they afford the offer?
- Are they the decision maker?
- If this is an event or program that requires their time, will they have the time to commit to this?

During the qualifying stage, you'll find all of this out before moving to the finale. This is where you truly connect with and understand the prospect on a deeper level. You'll do this by asking the right questions at the right time.

THE NEEDS GRADING SCALE

When you enter a call, you want to put your prospect on a needs grading scale. What is this grading scale? It's a scale to determine how much your prospect needs or wants the offer, and it ranges anywhere between one and ten: "one" meaning they don't need your offer at all and "ten" meaning they need your offer badly and urgently.

Why should we do this? Well, don't you think it would be a good idea to use different approaches for heavily invested prospects versus the curious tire kickers? Different needs will need different strategies.

The grading scale looks like this:

- One through five means the prospect has low needs.
- Six through eight means they have some need or interest.
- Nine through ten means they have high interest, passion, or urgency.

Can you see why it's a bad idea to talk about money or close the deal if the prospect has a need that's only a grade of two? On the other hand, can you see why digging into someone's pains will be counter-productive if they are already a nine on the scale? By understanding and gauging where the prospect is at regarding their degree of pain, you'll have a clearer idea of when to move on.

You only want to move on to the last stage of the call when you've moved the prospect to a rating of eight or above. When the needs are low (below five), you want to ask strategic questions to bring their needs up. A good strategic question makes the prospect think and allows them to come to their logical conclusions.

HIGH-TICKET CLOSER® EXAMPLE:

Closer: "How much revenue are you currently generating?"

Prospect: "About 100k a month."

Closer: "100k? That's pretty good. What's wrong with that?"

Prospect: "Well, we aren't as profitable as we'd like to be."

Now you might be wondering what's so special about a simple question like that. Well, compare it to how a typical salesperson might have approached that same conversation.

TYPICAL SALESPERSON EXAMPLE:

Salesperson: "How much revenue are you currently generating?"

Prospect: "About 100k a month."

Salesperson: "Well, with your business model, that can't be too profitable. Here's what you should do, and here's how we can help."

Do you see the difference? It's subtle, but it makes all the difference in the world when it comes to results. There are many types of questions to ask; here's a list of common questions you can use to gather more information:

- "I'm sure that's working well for you. What's wrong with that?"
- "Exactly what kind of results are you looking for?"

- "What would change in your life if you were living this type of dream?"
- "So, what are your goals? What are you trying to accomplish here?"
- "What do you think the problem is? What's stopping you?"
- "What has changed in your situation recently?"
- "Why do you feel you need the help now?"

Once you have properly qualified the prospect for needs, desires, money, and decision-making, you can move onto the last stage of the call—Commitment.

STAGE THREE: THE COMMITMENT

After you've finished the qualifying stage, the commitment stage happens when you present the offer, ask for the commitment, verify why it's so important, and seal the deal.

In this section, it's all about getting the prospect to commit to the sale. It's about getting them to decide for themselves that this is the right choice. Remember, when you say something, it means something; when the prospect says something, it means everything. Usually, typical salespeople at this stage will try to stack the value and make it look like a great deal for the prospect, but that's not how High-Ticket Closers® move toward the close.

HIGH-TICKET CLOSER® EXAMPLE:

Closer: "So, Mr. Prospect, I know that you wanted X, Y, and Z today. However, there are so many other companies out there who are cheaper than us; why did you want to work with us?"

Prospect: "Well, you have a really good reputation, and all my friends have told me you deliver great work. So I could see us generating lots of profit if we worked with you."

Closer: "Great. So where should we go from here?"

Prospect: "Let's do this."

Compare this to the typical salesperson's approach.

TYPICAL SALESPERSON EXAMPLE:

Salesperson: "So, with our package, you'll get A, B, and C. On top of all that, we'll add in D. Usually that would cost you $10,000, but for fast action takers like you we can do $7,500. So, would you like to buy today?"

Prospect: "Um ... let me think about it."

Salesperson: "What's there to think about?"

And that's it—those are the three simple stages of a High-Ticket Closing® call. When you structure your calls this way, you'll find yourself staying grounded and in control instead of jumping around from topic to topic. You'll find yourself having to deal with fewer objections and that your calls go more smoothly than ever before.

WHAT'S NEXT?

At this point, you might be overwhelmed from what you've just learned, or you might be wondering what a High Ticket Closing® call sounds like in action.

If you want to learn more about High-Ticket Closing®, go to unlockitbook.com/resources. There you will find live role plays of calls, receive extra training, and see what it's like to be a High-Ticket Closer®.

Now that you've learned about High-Ticket Closing®, you've unlocked a powerful way to convert prospects into customers. But remember, sales are just one part of the equation. In the next chapter, you'll learn the core components to unlocking your business growth.

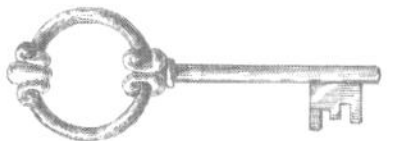

CHAPTER 8

Unlock Your Business Growth

IDEAL FOR: **THE CASTAWAY, UNFULFILLED KING**

Most entrepreneurs leave their rat race only to find themselves running on a hamster wheel. They're "hustling." They're putting out fires and applying BAND-AID® solutions. They're stuck in a "feast or famine" cycle and constantly concerned about finding the next sale, the next customer. They can't operate effectively as an entrepreneur as they are always reacting and are never proactive.

It's no wonder why half of small businesses fail within the first five years, according to the Small Business Administration. The question is: how you can set up the core structure of your business so it can grow, scale, and remain sane?

THE THREE PILLARS OF BUSINESS GROWTH

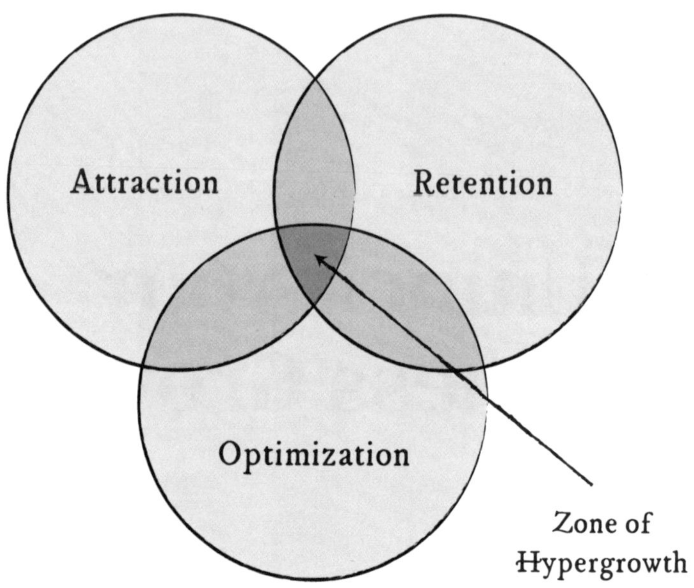

When you look at it, there are only three ways to unlock your business growth. What are these three ways? Here they are.

- **ATTRACTION**: Being able to predictably and consistently attract new quality leads and generate new business
- **RETENTION**: Increasing stick rate of each customer and enhancing the relationship customers have with your business
- **OPTIMIZATION**: Maximizing the value your business generates for the customer

Most struggling businesses are weak in either one or a blend of these three pillars. As you'll see, these pillars work together to create a strong, sustainable, and scalable business. If any of these pillars are weak, you're looking at an unbalanced business.

ATTRACTION: HOW TO PREDICTABLY, PROFITABLY, AND CONSISTENTLY ATTRACT YOUR IDEAL CUSTOMERS

No company ever goes out of business for having too much revenue. Most businesses struggle because they lack revenue. They struggle because they can't predictably generate new business. While revenue does not solve all your business problems, revenue can solve many problems.

Attraction can be broken down into two phases: marketing and closing. Marketing is creating top-of-mind awareness and generating new leads for your business. Closing is turning those leads from prospects into a sale. Put together, Attraction is all about creating a predictable, profitable, and consistent way of generating new customers. The first step to achieve this is to figure out:

How much can you afford to spend to acquire a customer?

For most business owners, they have no clue. They think to themselves, "Well, I want customers for as little as possible." They rely on referrals, networking, cold calling, "hustle," and sweat equity and then find that their business isn't growing. They don't realize the reason they aren't growing and are struggling is that you cannot control referrals.

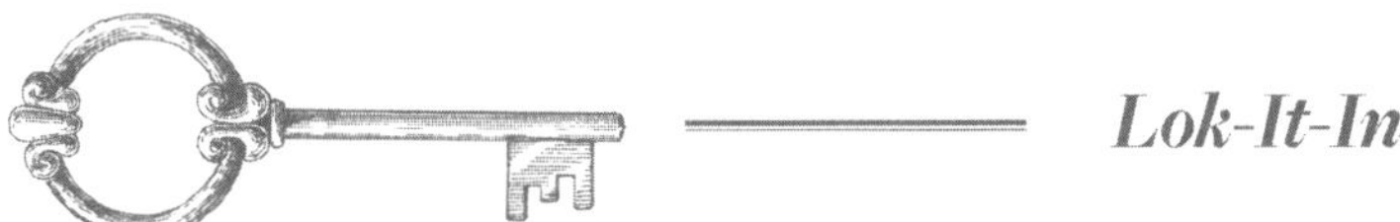

Lok-It-In

UNLESS YOU HAVE A PREDICTABLE, CONSISTENT WAY OF ATTRACTING CUSTOMERS, YOU DON'T HAVE A BUSINESS—YOU HAVE A HOBBY.

Many business owners don't mind relying on referrals and are proud to say that they spend no money on marketing. What they don't realize is that if you rely on referrals for growth, then you're operating your business on blind faith. If you don't have a predictable system for acquiring customers, then you don't have a business—you have a hobby. However, once you decide on what you're willing to spend to acquire a customer, your marketing becomes simple math.

MARKETING IS MATH

Let's say you are selling a product that's worth $1,000 and the cost of goods sold is $200. You are selling an $800 product. How much are you going to reallocate back into the business? Most entrepreneurs will say "as little as possible"—they want to keep as much profit as possible. I have a different philosophy. I want to outspend all my competitors to acquire a customer. Here's why.

Imagine two businesses: Business A and Business B. Business A is only willing to spend $100 to acquire a customer, while Business B spends $500 to acquire a customer. Who do you think will win? When you can outspend your competition to acquire a customer, you can scale more aggressively and advertise on more channels. You have more market share, more market penetration, and more top-of-mind awareness than your competition. In the end, whoever can spend the most money to acquire a customer wins.

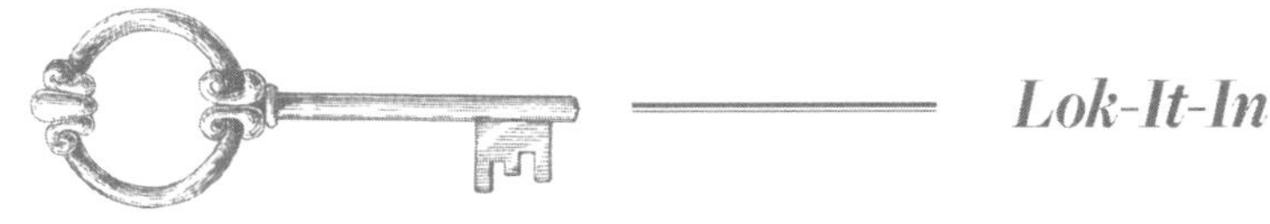

Lok-It-In

WHOEVER CAN SPEND THE MOST MONEY TO ACQUIRE A CUSTOMER WINS.

Now how do you decide on the amount you're willing to spend on acquiring a customer? For my team, our allowable cost per acquisition is 70 percent of the initial purchase. Meaning if my offer was $1,000, I'd be okay with spending $700 to acquire that customer. After multiple rounds of testing and refining, this is the number we've decided on that works for our business. Yours may be different.

We are okay with spending that much on acquiring a customer because most of our profits are made in the back end when we give our customers the option to upgrade to higher-end or recurring offers.

RETENTION: TURNING CUSTOMERS INTO RAVING FANS

Retention can be broken down into two parts. One is about customer satisfaction, and the other is about customer ascension.

CUSTOMER SATISFACTION

As you grow as an entrepreneur, it becomes too easy to disconnect from your customers and to lose focus on their experience. Keeping a pulse on the customers' perception of your business is critical for business growth.

Our team reviews our Net Promoter Score (NPS) on a consistent basis to make sure customer satisfaction is met. Here's how it works: simply ask your customers to rate you from one to ten on this question:

"How likely are you to recommend our product/service to a friend or colleague?

Your customers will fall into one of three categories:

- Promoters—if they pick nine or ten
- Passives—if they pick seven or eight
- Detractors—if they pick anywhere from zero to six

Your NPS will be the percentage of Promoters minus the percentage of Detractors. For example, if you have 60 percent Promoters and 10 percent Detractors, your NPS would be fifty. If you hit above seventy, that's considered world class. Our team aims for and regularly hits ninety—and if we miss that mark, we adjust quickly. What's the secret to achieving high NPS scores? It's elevating the customers to higher levels of loyalty—customer ascension.

CUSTOMER ASCENSION

Do you believe all customers are created the same? I don't. Not every customer will have the same relationship with you and your business. Some will turn out to be much more profitable than the others. If you want to grow your business, focus on the customers with whom you have a decent relationship.

There are five levels of relationship you can have with your customers. These levels range from prospect to raving fan. They are in order from most to least loyal:

1. Raving Fan
2. Member
3. Client
4. Customer
5. Prospect

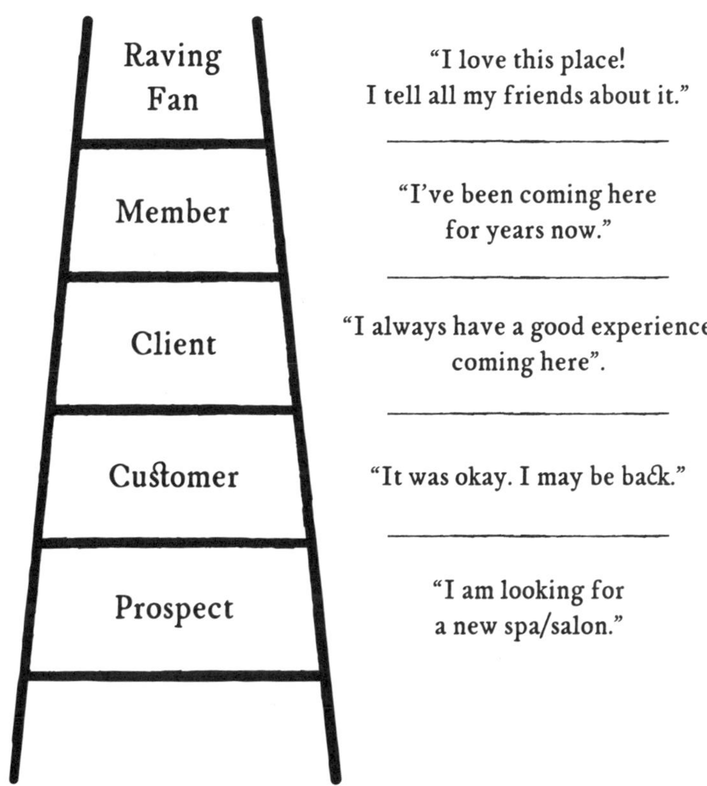

The raving fan loves your business and tells all their friends about it. The member is a loyal customer who buys from you consistently and frequently. The client comes occasionally, but always has a pleasant experience with you. The customer buys from you once, and they might come back. The prospect is looking for a solution to their problem, and you're one of the options they're investigating.

Lok-It-In

THE RATE OF GROWTH IS DETERMINED BY HOW FAST YOU MOVE YOUR CUSTOMERS UP THE LOYALTY LADDER.

Your job is to move the prospect up the Loyalty Ladder—turning your prospects into raving fans and members.

CUSTOMERS VS. MEMBERS

Why do you want to focus on members over customers? The first reason is that people who see themselves as members buy 66.3 percent more than those who see themselves as just customers, according to Tim Schmidt from Tribal Marketing. Second, members give you recurring and predictable revenue without having to spend more on acquiring new customers. Lastly, even with all the benefits you get from acquiring members over customers, the costs to acquire a customer are the same as acquiring a member.

The relationship you have with members is much stronger as well. Customers are short term and care about the products and services they seek. Members are long term and care about the human connection and philosophy that comes with your product or service.

Strong memberships are at the core of what's built successful businesses around the world—Amazon Prime, Costco, CrossFit, Netflix, Starbucks—these companies are all built on the backbone of strong memberships. When you have a strong membership, you'll have a strong foundation for long-term growth.

MEMBERSHIPS ARE BUILT ON COMMUNITY

Here's a fun experiment you can try. Go and try to convince someone from CrossFit that LA Fitness is a better company. If you know anyone who is into CrossFit, you'll know that's an impossible task. No matter what type of argument you throw at them, they won't change their mind. It's all because of one word: "community."

CrossFit has its community, its own culture. The people on the inside feel as if they are part of a close, tight-knit family—while the people on the outside have no idea why CrossFit members are so passionate. That's the effect of having a strong community.

When you have a strong community, the members of the community will advocate for your business without any incentive. If you have a strong community, your business will become a part of who they are, and they will fight for you. They will gladly pay to stay in the community, they'll anticipate every product you send into the market, and they'll represent your brand proudly and loudly. The fact is you don't need large amounts of capital to lay down the foundation of a strong community. All you need are these three steps:

1. KNOW YOUR VALUES

To know your values is an essential thing in your community. What does your community stand for, and what does it not stand for? What do you believe, and what do you not believe? Why does your community exist? Apple exists to challenge the status quo and attracts those people while repelling the people who want to go with the flow. What values will your community value?

2. OVERDELIVER ON YOUR PROMISE

Most businesses will deliver on what they promised in the offer (and some may underdeliver), but almost no business will go out of their way to overdeliver for their customers and members. Zappos was the first company to offer free shipping on both orders and returns—giving their customers a "wow" experience. Many questioned their practice because it cost the company money every time someone returned a product; however, what they didn't realize was the loyalty Zappos gained by overdelivering. How can you overdeliver for your members?

3. CREATE A SPACE FOR MEMBERS TO CONNECT

Members of a community want to meet and connect. Humans have a natural tendency to seek out other people who are like minded and have the same values. My students—the High-Ticket Closers®—interact daily with one another online and share their booms (their wins) as well as their challenges. On top of that, we have an exclusive annual black-tie event where thousands of closers fly into Vancouver to meet with one another. What's one way you can help your members connect?

Now that you understand the power of retention and membership, there is one last pillar that will give your business a boost in growth—optimization.

OPTIMIZATION: HOW TO MAXIMIZE THE VALUE OF EVERY CUSTOMER

Optimization is all about maximizing the value of each customer in your business. At any time percent of your customers are willing and want to buy more from you—they need the right offers presented to them.

Here's an example of one of my company's sales funnels:

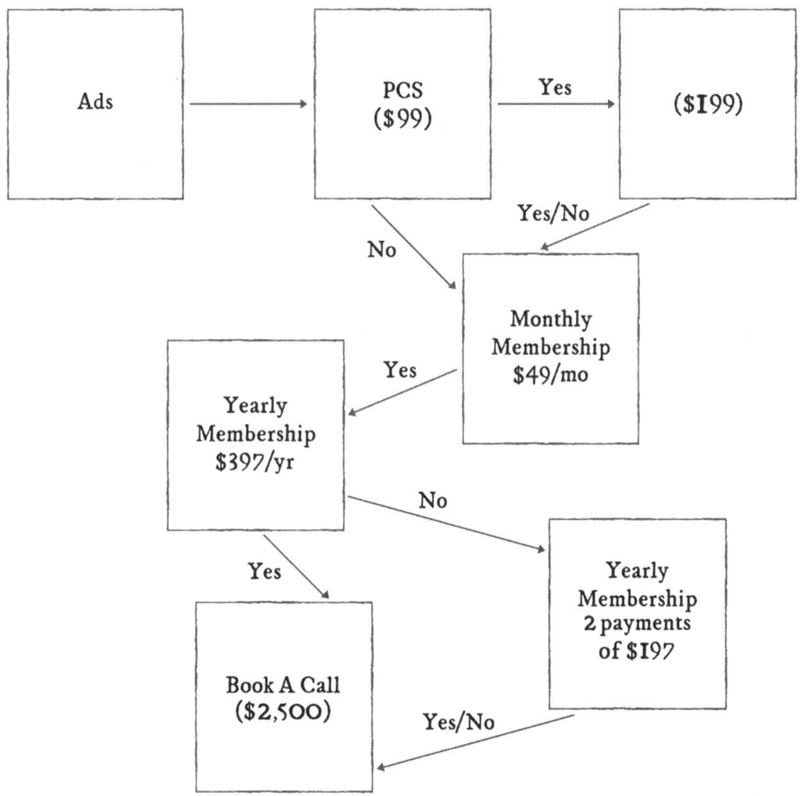

On the front end, there is a $99 offer made to the prospect. (This is one of our products called Perfect Closing Script, a compelling script that helps salespeople improve their closing ratio.) If they take the offer, they're given another opportunity to purchase a one-time offer for $199—this is a product that complements the initial purchase. If they do not take the offer, they're brought to a down sell for a $49 monthly membership we offer to people who need to train their closing skills.

For the customers who buy our $99 product, about 15 to 20 percent take the $199 offer. That means 15 to 20 percent of customers are now worth $298 instead of the initial $99. The customers who buy our $49 membership are given an option to pay in full for an annual membership for $397—a 10 percent upgrade to annual membership right away. If they don't want to pay in full, they're given another option to split the yearly investment into two payments.

Finally, at the end of the sales funnel they can book a call with one of my closers who will see if they're a good fit for our higher-end program at $2,500. (When this program is sold over the phone it converts at 25 to 32 percent.) By the end of the sales funnel, many of our customers have invested much more than the initial $99. About one-fifth of the customers take the $199 offer, another 15 percent join our membership, and one-fifth of the remaining customers take the $2,500 offer. That means instead of having customers worth only $99, we have customers with lifetime values of $298 and $2,798—along with recurring revenue made from memberships. This is just one example of optimization.

On top of the upsells, we retarget all nonbuyers with ads on Facebook, YouTube, Instagram, and other platforms—bringing them back to book a call with our closers. With all the money we put into our social advertising and product funnels, why do we bring them to a sales call? Because we've found that selling High-Ticket Offers over the phone converts five times better than any other medium of selling. We'll talk more about that in the next chapter.

When you are working on optimization, ask yourself these questions:

- What else could you offer them that would complement what they just purchased?
- What type of problem are they likely going to face NEXT? How can you help them?
- How can you deliver more value so you can raise your prices?
- Could you turn this one-time purchase into a repeat purchase (membership)?

THE KEY TO UNLOCKING YOUR BUSINESS GROWTH

When you strengthen the three pillars of Attraction, Retention, and Optimization, you'll unlock your business growth and create a business where you:

- Have a predictable, consistent, and profitable way of acquiring customers
- Can turn customers into members, and members into raving fans
- Maximize the value to you of each customer who comes through the doors

Once you have these three strong pillars, there will be one more crucial component to consider as you scale your business: your profit margins.

CHAPTER 9

Unlock Your Profit Margins

IDEAL FOR: **CASTAWAY AND THE UNFULFILLED KING/QUEEN**

Is more always better? When I talk with entrepreneurs, many of them are always focused on more—more sales, more customers, more employees, more growth, more infrastructure, more scaling, more this, more that, more, more, more! But is more better?

When entrepreneurs focus too much on getting more without questioning why, I always think back to this particular episode of *The Profit*—a reality TV show where the star of the show, Marcus Lemonis, comes in and tries to save small businesses from failure.

In this episode, he was trying to save a family business (a meat-packing company) that's been in business for over seventy-five years.

They were generating $50 million in revenue per year! Is that a lot of money? Of course. If that's all you knew, you'd probably ask yourself why this company needed saving. When you take a look at their other numbers, you start to see the full story.

Though they had $50 million in revenue, their net profit was negative $400,000. They were losing $400,000 every year. On top of that, they were $4 million in debt. When you only focus on the revenue and growth of the company, you can be easily deceived.

The only thing that matters in running a business is net profit. Businesses go bankrupt because they run out of cash—and you cannot have any cash left if you don't make any profits.

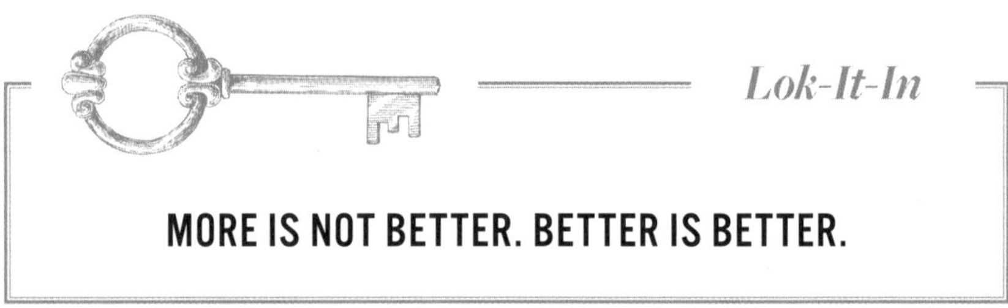

On top of that, when you have low-profit margins, here's what also happens:

- You can't deliver a great experience for your customers.
- You have to go cheap in certain areas of your business to minimize expense (that's why you can't deliver a great experience).
- Your growth is restricted because you can't spend to acquire customers.
- You're forced to compete on price.
- You're at a disadvantage against competitors who have higher margins.

- Your room for error is tiny—no margin means no buffer room for mistakes.
- You don't have enough money to attract the best talent, the best people.
- Your customers don't value you or your product/service.
- You need a higher volume of customers to meet your revenue and profit goals.
- Any new customer you acquire makes very little difference to your bottom line.

With low-profit margins, you're at a huge disadvantage. You can't buy the supplies you need; you can't hire skilled and talented employees. You can't even support yourself. It's not sustainable, it's not scalable, and it puts you in a very dangerous position.

Some business owners are so naive and delusional, they think that if there's gross enough, then there must be some net somewhere. I was one of those entrepreneurs. I learned these lessons the hard way and didn't want you to make the same mistake. I've learned the hard way that you cannot multiply zero. I've learned the hard way that business is a game of margins, not volume.

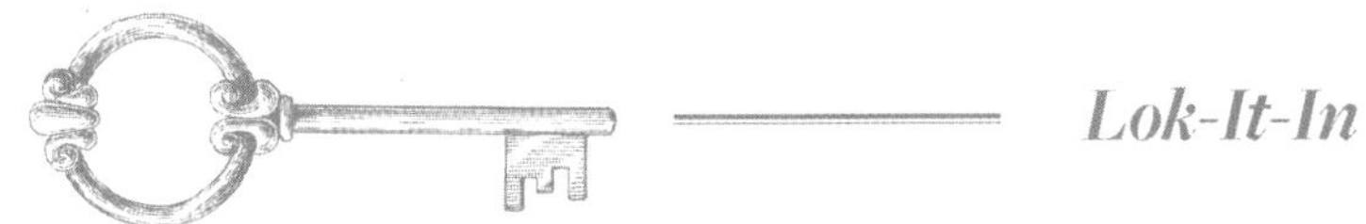

BUSINESS IS A GAME OF MARGINS, NOT VOLUME.

THREE REASONS WHY SELLING HIGH TICKET MAKES SENSE

When you sell High-Ticket Offers, you're making a larger profit margin. You're not only giving yourself more room to breathe, but you're also giving yourself more opportunity for growth. Your ability to scale quickly and profitably, the depth of relationships you have with your customers, the type of business you run and the lifestyle you live—they're all directly shaped by your decision to sell High-Ticket Offers.

REASON #1: SCALE FASTER BY OUTSPENDING YOUR COMPETITORS

Picture this. You're running a business that sells one product for $30, and it costs $5 to produce and fulfill—you're left with $25 profit.

$30 price - $5 cost = $25 profit

To acquire a customer, you have $25 as your marketing budget. That means you can spend only up to $25 to acquire a new customer or else you'd be losing money with each sale.

Any platform you choose to advertise on—whether it's TV, radio, billboards, YouTube, Facebook, Instagram, Google, or some other platform—you can't spend over $25 to acquire a customer. Even organic sales will only give you a maximum profit of $25.

With such a small margin, you won't be able to scale, and your room for error is tiny. If your ad costs rise, you won't have the time or resources to adjust—you'll be left out to dry. If you wanted to invest in better talent or improve your infrastructure, you wouldn't have any money to pull from—your margins are gone.

Compare this to another business selling a single product at

$5,000. Let's say their total costs are $500. Profit is $4,500.

$5,000 price - $500 cost = $4,500 profit

If this business competes with the business with $25 margin, who do you think will win? The one with a higher profit margin. Whoever can outspend their competition to acquire a customer wins. In this case, $4,500 beats $25. With higher profit margins, you can advertise on more platforms, more channels, and test more ways of converting a customer.

Now, does this mean you shouldn't sell low-ticket offers at all? No—but the ONLY reason you will see a low-ticket offer is to bring buyers into the door. That way you could upsell them other High-Ticket Offers. However, keep in mind that this is a strategy, not a business model.

REASON #2: SIMPLER BUSINESS, HAPPIER LIFE

Forget what everyone else says: size matters. We're talking about transaction size. There are many ways to make money, but how you make money is as important as how much money you make.

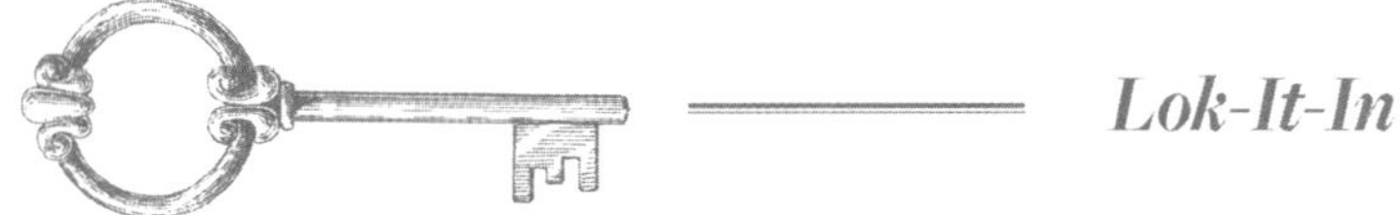

Lok-It-In

IT'S NOT HOW MUCH MONEY YOU MAKE; IT'S HOW YOU MAKE MONEY.

Different Ways To Make A Million Dollars

$1	x	1,000,000 customers	= $1,000,000
$10	x	100,000 customers	= $1,000,000
$25	x	40,000 customers	= $1,000,000
$150	x	4,000 customers	= $1,000,000
$2,500	x	400 customers	= $1,000,000
$10,000	x	100 customers	= $1,000,000
$100,000	x	10 customers	= $1,000,000
$1,000,000	x	1 customer	= $1,000,000

There are many different ways to make a million dollars. However, is there a difference between having one hundred thousand customers versus one hundred customers? You bet.

Your customer support, your team, your infrastructure need to be in place to handle one hundred thousand customers, or else your business will collapse on itself. Plus, if you want to grow to one million customers, you'll need to reinvent everything. The systems that can handle one thousand customers won't be able to handle one hundred thousand customers. The systems created for one hundred thousand customers won't support one million customers—what got you here won't get you there.

Now there's nothing wrong with building a business with low-ticket prices and a high volume of customers, but I prefer to keep things simple and profitable. If you want to multiply effectively and with minimum "growing pains," you must simplify. A business with a simple offer and fewer customers will have a much better time scaling sustainably.

REASON #3: WORK ONLY WITH IDEAL CUSTOMERS

Not all customers are the same. You see, there are four types of customers—some you want to market to; some you don't.

CHEAP	SOPHISTICATED
DIFFICULT	AFFLUENT

CHEAP CUSTOMERS

They're very demanding and buy purely on price—they do not understand value. Usually, the first question they ask you is, "How much do you charge?" before they even understand what you are offering. They're the customers who will ask you for deals and discounts.

DIFFICULT CUSTOMERS

These customers aren't necessarily cheap, but they're just difficult. They're generally negative and downers. They're the customers who will have unrealistically high expectations of what you are selling. If you run a client-based business, these customers will ask you a million irrelevant questions and call you at 3:00 a.m.

SOPHISTICATED CUSTOMERS

These customers are educated and know what they want. They've done their research ahead of time and have already talked to a few people. If they walk into a car shop, they'll know the exact model, color, features, and payment plan they want. Sometimes, these customers will need more time to think before making a decision—but once they make up their mind, they stick to their decision.

AFFLUENT CUSTOMERS

These customers buy based on feelings and emotions. If they can afford it and they want it, they will buy it. These customers don't want deals or discounts—they think it cheapens what they're buying. If there is a discount, their immediate thought is something is wrong with the product.

When you take a look at these four types of customers, which ones would you want to have for your business? If you're like most people, you'd want to stay away from the cheap and difficult customers, and you'd probably want to serve the sophisticated and affluent customers.

Why? Because when there's an economic downturn, the first groups of customers affected are cheap and challenging customers. They didn't have much disposable income to begin with—so if there is a choice to be made between rent and your product, chances are they will choose rent.

It makes intuitive sense, yet most businesses unknowingly structure their business to attract cheap and demanding customers. They advertise discounts and deals to drive more sales. They do everything and bend over backward to get a customer. They think that if they take on a cheap customer and overdeliver, that customer will eventually pay more. (They never do.)

I've structured my business to repel cheap and demanding customers. I'd much rather spend time with sophisticated and affluent customers. Your selling price influences what type of customer you'll attract—low prices attract budget-concerned customers; premium prices attract quality-concerned customers.

When you charge premium prices, it becomes a better experience for your customers as well. They appreciate what they've bought, complain less, and feel they've gotten more value—and it enhances their relationship with you. So with all these reasons for selling High Ticket, why do so many business owners undercharge? Well, there are many reasons, but there are three pervasive myths that keep entrepreneurs from selling High-Ticket Offers.

THREE MYTHS THAT PREVENT ENTREPRENEURS FROM CHARGING PREMIUM PRICES

MYTH #1: I'LL LOSE ALL MY CUSTOMERS IF I RAISE MY PRICE

This myth comes from a misunderstanding of what matters to a customer. There is the price (how much something costs), and then there's the value (what you get in relation to what you paid for). When you raise your prices, you'll attract customers who see the value of your offer. However, you'll repel the customers who only look at the price.

When you have low prices, you'll attract the price shopper who is always looking for bargains—the ones who will negotiate until they're blue in the face to get the lowest price. When you have premium prices, you'll attract a loyal, long-term client who's willing to pay a higher price to get what they want. By increasing your rate, you'll attract a different market of customers.

Yes, you will "lose" the price shoppers and bargain hunters—but do you want to build your business off of customers who are always looking to pay the least possible? When you live by price, you die by price.

MYTH #2: "COMPETITIVE PRICING"

Once I was invited for an interview on a show alongside an economics professor. The host of the show asked, "How should you price your offers?" The professor went on to say something along the lines of, "Well, you've got to do your marketplace research and see what everyone else is charging. Then you'll have a good idea of what to charge yourself."

I disagreed. I asked them, "What does my competition have to do with me?" If the value I offer is different from my competition, shouldn't my price be different as well? There's no reason to copy their price. What if my competition has lousy marketing, poorly packaged offers, and horrible messaging? Should I copy that as well?"

My competition doesn't get to dictate my price or anything I do in my business. When you compete on price with your competitors, it becomes a race to the bottom, and no one wins. Even if you do get more customers by lowering your price, do you want to have the reputation of being the "cheapest"? You announce what you're worth to the world. If your value to the marketplace is unique, your price should be too.

Don't let your consumers compare you like apples to apples; let them compare apples to oranges. You don't want to be seen as a commodity—when you're a commodity, you're the same as everyone else and easily replaceable.

MYTH #3: SELLING AT HIGH-TICKET PRICES IS MORE DIFFICULT

What if I told you that selling a $10,000 offer takes the same amount of effort as selling a $1,000 offer? What if I told you that, sometimes, it's easier to sell a $10,000 offer over a $1,000 offer? The logic seems to go against conventional beliefs, but it's the truth. When you are selling High-Ticket Offers, you are selling to the sophisticated and affluent buyers, and they have a different mind-set when it comes to buying. They are not looking at the price; they are looking at value. Sophisticated buyers are asking, "Does this solve my problem?" and affluent buyers are asking, "Will this purchase make me feel good?" These buyers are not looking for discounts. They want the best that money can buy. That's why they're easier to sell than customers who purchase lower-ticket items. They understand the value of high-quality products and services.

Most people resist my suggestion that they raise their prices (I opposed raising rates myself in my copywriting business), but this resistance never has anything to do with their customers. All the price resistance comes from the seller, not the buyer. You see, people project their values onto others—they think, "If I'm not willing to pay for this at this price, then no one else will either." This couldn't be further from the truth.

If you're targeting the right market, the price will become elastic. When you can deliver a great buying experience, your customers will "stretch" to premium prices without resistance. People will always pay a premium price for a premium experience—only a small percentage of your customers buy purely based on price. When you understand that sophisticated customers buy to solve a specific problem and affluent customers buy to satisfy a deep emotion, you'll start to see that selling High-Ticket Offers is much easier than expected.

HOW TO SELL HIGH-TICKET OFFERS AT PREMIUM PRICES

When you change your offer, you change your life.

The steps to changing your offer are simple, and you don't even need to change what you're doing. Instead, change whom you're selling to, position yourself differently, package what you do differently, and focus on solving an urgent and important problem for your customers.

You have a choice. Do you want to be the Mercedes, the Toyota, or the Rolls Royce of your market? There's no wrong answer. I'm just saying that you need to know your business model. When I tell people to upgrade their offer, the "how to" steps are simple—but what holds them back is fear.

"Nobody will pay me that price"—fear of rejection.

"What if it doesn't work"—fear of failure.

"I have all the wrong people wanting to hear about my service"—fear of not being enough.

They are afraid of losing a bunch of customers, fearful of pissing people off, scared of failing; but from where does all this fear come? One word—"scarcity." Scarcity is holding them back. The truth is when you raise your prices, you'll lose a small 10 to 20 percent of your customers.

For most businesses, this would be catastrophic, as they have no way of dealing with that loss.

Imagine if you had so many customers lining up for what you're selling and were so in demand that you had a waiting list—would you be scared then? You wouldn't be. When you are in high demand, you won't be worried about losing customers. The key is to have abundance. The key is to have the power of supply and demand working in your favor. How do you do this? Through what I call Social Capital—meaning you create a following of people who like you, trust you, and will gladly buy from you.

CHAPTER 10

Unlock Your Social Capital

IDEAL FOR: **CASTAWAY AND UNFULFILLED KING/QUEEN**

The world is noisier than ever, the marketplace is more uncertain than ever, and it's more complicated than ever to get your customers' attention. You are not safe—no one is safe. Power has shifted from being in the hands of companies to the hands of consumers. Consumers today have more control than ever—they can skip TV ads, tune out radio ads, drive past your billboards, and ignore any attempt to enter their awareness.

Times were different back then. Imagine what it was like when a few large companies had access to all the mass media. You'd watch your favorite TV show, and a commercial would pop up, then you'd have no choice but to sit through the commercial. It's become more difficult than ever to grab attention. It's not that your customers don't trust you; they don't even know you exist.

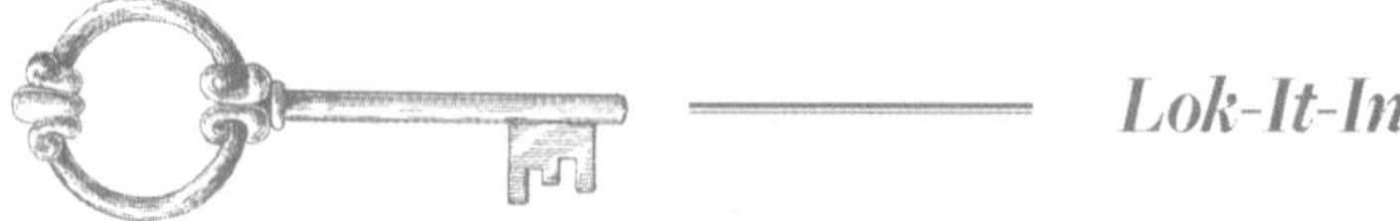

IT'S NO LONGER THE BIG FISH THAT EATS THE SMALL FISH. IT'S THE FAST FISH THAT EATS THE SLOW FISH.

Consumers today want what they want when they want it, where they want it, and how they want it. They could be watching YouTube on their TVs, bingeing TV shows on their iPads, or catching a game on their iPhones. If you can't adapt to market what they want where and when they are engaged, you'll fall behind, and you'll fall hard.

Giants can fall harder and faster. Victoria's Secret sales are plummeting after dominating the market. Sears has shut down hundreds of stores across the country. Nokia, Sony, Blockbuster, Yahoo, JCPenney—all these companies thought they were safe but failed to adapt to changing times. Whether you'll survive is determined by how fast you can learn, pivot, and adjust. It's no longer the big fish eating the small fish—it's the fast fish eating the slow fish.

FINANCIAL CAPITAL IS NOT THE MOST VALUABLE FORM OF CAPITAL

Financial capital is no longer the most valuable capital. Look at venture capital firms—they're having trouble finding start-ups that merit investment. Start-ups are bootstrapping and becoming more resourceful as they start—they are delaying and rejecting funding from venture capitalists to maintain equity and control of their company.

If you only have financial capital, all you have is dead money. You are not creating new value with the money; it's just lying around. When you have financial capital, you are thinking, "How can I put it to good use?" You're debating whether to invest in new people, upgrade your infrastructure, scale your marketing, or one of a hundred other actions. But on its own, financial capital is NOT the most valuable form of capital. What IS valuable is a form of capital that allows you to multiply financial capital—it's called Social Capital.

THE RISE OF SOCIAL CAPITAL

You might have heard the saying that "attention is the new currency"—that's only partially true. Attention itself is not a form of currency—the right attention from the right people is the new currency. Getting your customer's attention is part of the equation, but you can't just get attention for attention's sake. After all, any idiot could run around in the street, scream at the top of their lungs, and get attention. Any company can create a flashy ad to raise "brand awareness," but would this build long-term relationships with your customers?

There are Instagram celebrities that have over two million followers, but struggle to sell even thirty-six T-shirts. They have a huge social following, but they are still broke. I am not interested in having a social following; I only have a social following so I can create social capital.

Social capital is a following of people who like you, trust you, support you, and are willing and capable of buying from you.

It's the key to strategically scaling—the ability to create massive growth in revenue and profits without adding enormous costs. Social capital is not just a social following. Social capital can be turned into financial capital in the form of sales and customers. It can also be turned into relational capital in the form of connections, relationships, partnerships, and strategic alliances.

Think about it—how did Kylie Jenner become the youngest billionaire at the age of twenty-one? Is it because she pumped in millions of dollars of venture capital and outside funding into her cosmetic line? No. The reason she could create so much wealth at such a staggering speed is that she has spent years building a huge reserve of social capital, and when she converted this reserve into financial capital, she accomplished a feat that no other company in history had accomplished.

Kylie Jenner might have been the first to do this, but she definitely won't be the last. We are entering an age where social capital is becoming more important than ever. It's why start-ups can turn down venture capital—they're learning how to build their businesses on the foundation of social capital.

Take Dollar Shave Club. As a small start-up with no outside funding, they launched their commercial, which has now been viewed over twenty-five million times on YouTube. In 2016, Unilever bought Dollar Shave Club for $1 billion—unheard of in their industry. Why did Unilever pay such a large amount? They responded, "It's not about the revenue. It's about relationships." They saw the value of their social capital.

TURNING YOUR SOCIAL CAPITAL INTO AN INFINITE WELL

When done correctly, social capital can become an infinite well that you can draw from again and again. The problem is that most people don't understand that social capital is like a bank—you can't withdraw what you have not deposited.

The common mistake most companies make with social media is that they try to sell to their customers with every interaction without delivering value first. When customers see these companies, they're thinking, "Oh, what are they going to try to sell me this time?"

Somehow, people think this is okay. Imagine going into a bank and trying to withdraw when you have nothing in the account—there's a word for that: it's called "robbery."

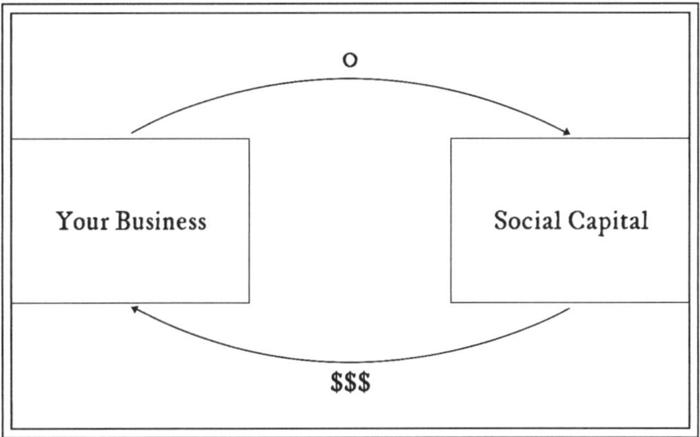

On the other hand, some companies have a good balance of depositing into their followers and withdrawing from their social capital. They focus on having a balanced combination of branding (depositing) and sales (withdrawal). This works, but it's not optimal. As a hedge against the worst-case scenario, responsible businesses will have a cash reserve in case things go wrong. If times turn bad, they'll have a cash reserve to meet payroll and expenses. It's the same with social capital.

You can deposit and withdraw at the same rate, but that's like putting $100 in and taking $100 out—you'll always be left with zero in the bank. If times get tough, you won't have anything to draw from—you won't have any social capital reserve.

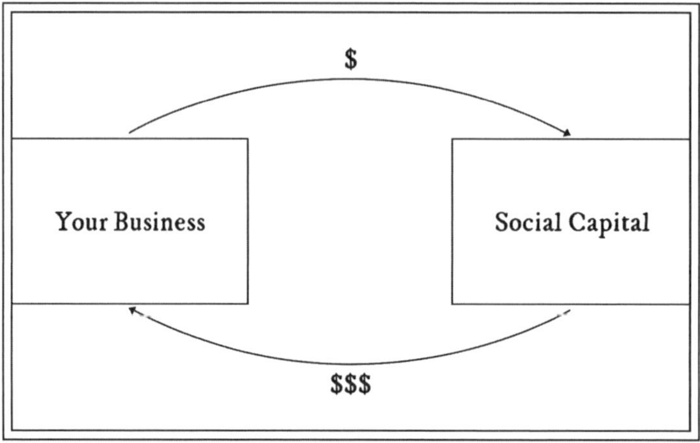

That's why I deposit more into my social capital than I withdraw. I make deposits into my social capital every single day. So when I want to convert my social capital into financial capital, it's simple and easy.

Since I've invested heavily in my social capital, everything else in my business has become easier. I sell my High-Ticket Offers without resistance—in fact, sometimes my closers must turn people down. On top of that, I've gained access to celebrities, met with high-level CEOs and founders, and formed highly profitable partnerships—all because of my social capital.

I could raise money if I want to, but I don't need to. However, let's suppose for fun, I were to launch a Kickstarter campaign—I could raise money overnight. I could turn my social capital into money if I needed to, and I wouldn't need to wait. Why is that? Because I've accumulated a substantial amount of social capital over the years.

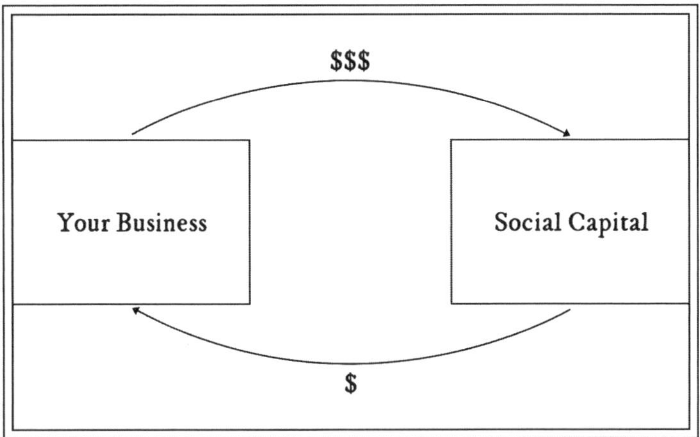

When you think of it this way, you can see how any platform becomes a bank for your social capital. Facebook is a bank, Instagram is a bank, YouTube is a bank, Google is a bank, traditional media is a bank, and media coverage is a bank.

Social capital is not monopolized by large TV networks anymore either. As of this writing, based on numbers aggregated on Statista, my YouTube channel alone has more subscribers than the viewers of MSNBC, ESPN, USA Network, TBS, TNT, Discovery, CNN, Food Network, and Nickelodeon, to name a few. The networks with viewers that exceed our subscribers are limited to the Fox News Channel, Fox, ABC, CBS, and NBC. This proves that you don't need to have your TV station to build your social capital—you can create your network.

DAN LOK'S YOUTUBE STATISTICS

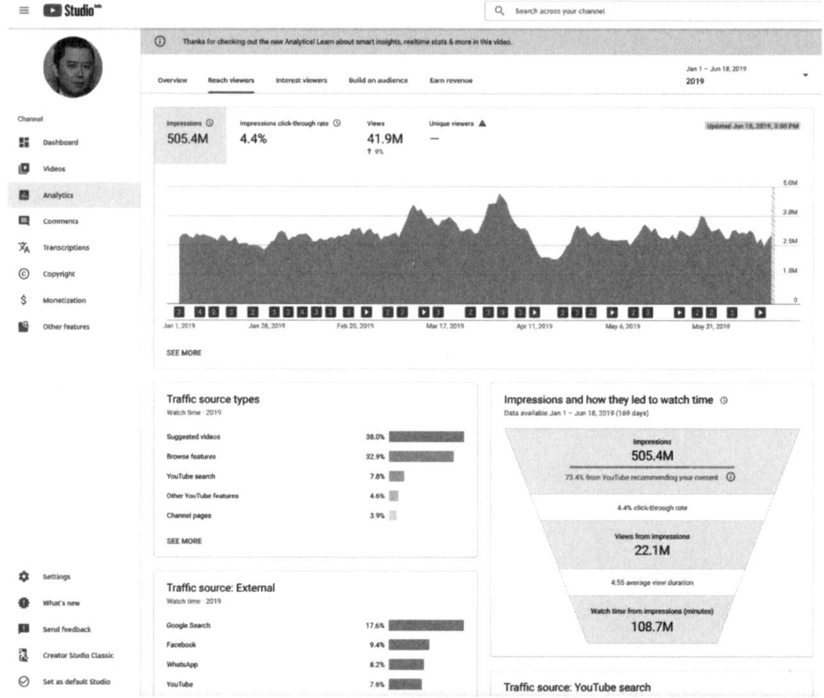

DAN LOK'S INSTAGRAM STATISTICS

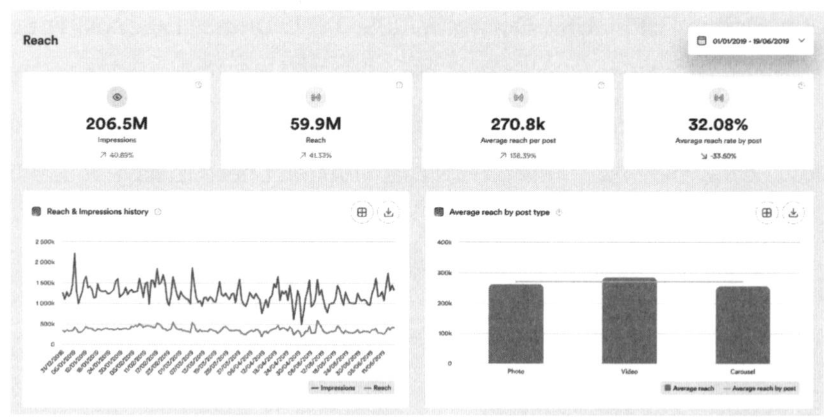

DAN LOK'S FACEBOOK STATISTICS

Without social capital, you are in danger. If you are a brand-new company, you don't exist unless you can cut through the noise. If you are an existing company, you're in trouble if you don't build that trust and relationship with your customers.

HOW TO SCALE AND MULTIPLY YOUR SOCIAL CAPITAL

The old way of selling is dead. Before, you could put up a couple of ads in front of a cold audience, drive them to a page, and expect them to buy. In the old days, this would be a profitable way of running a business. The days where you can put your offer in front of a cold audience with no priming, no context, no relationship, no value, and no trust are over. The cautious buyer is extremely selective in whom they trust and give loyalty.

That's why a new strategy is required to acquire and scale social capital. This is the same strategy I've used with my team to scale to over hundreds of millions of impressions across our platforms. Not only has this strategy expanded our social following, but it's the reason we've been able to scale our revenues and profits very quickly, consistently.

THE SOCIAL CAPITAL MULTIPLIER

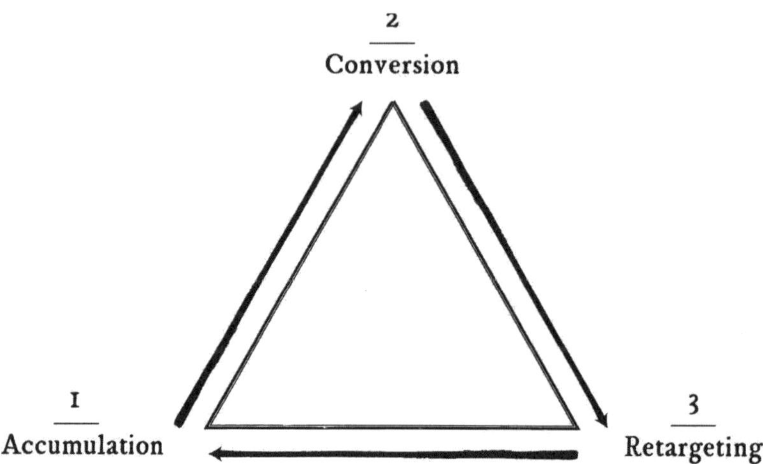

The Social Capital Multiplier is divided into three steps: Accumulation, Conversion, and Retargeting. Accumulation turns a cold audience into a warm audience. Conversion gets a commitment from your audience. Retargeting captures sales that were missed during the Conversion step.

ACCUMULATION: REVENUE THROUGH VALUE

The goals for the Accumulation step are:

- Build trust and start a relationship with your audience through delivering value
- Generate views and impressions
- Prime your audience for offers in the Conversion step

When you are selling High-Ticket Offers, there is a Theory of Consumption. The theory states that your customer must have consumed at least one hour of content for every thousand dollars they spend with you. That's why this step is so crucial.

In this step, you are delivering value to your audience and helping them solve a problem. You are giving them valuable content, and it's the first step toward building a relationship with them. There is no pitch, no selling, no closing—just value. If you go to my social media platforms, you'll see thousands of educational videos and content designed to help my audience, both paid and organic content. It would be best if you were actively spending to get your message to new segments of the market. Once they consume your content, they will be primed for the Conversion step—and you'll generate leads at a lower cost. I used to spend $5 to acquire a lead from a cold audience. Today, I only pay $0.15 with this strategy. This gives me the advantage—by allocating 50 percent of our budget to Accumulation, I'm able to acquire leads for pennies on the dollar.

CONVERSION: ACQUIRING LEADS FOR PENNIES ON THE DOLLAR

The goal for the Conversion step is to:

- Convert prospects into a lead or a customer to get a commitment from the prospect

I do not put offers in front of audiences that do not know who I am. Every person who is presented with an offer is primed and receptive before seeing the offer. On Facebook, you can see who's watched certain percentages of your video. On YouTube, you can tell who has seen your videos. In any media platform, you'll have a way of knowing who has viewed your content and how to target them.

Once you know who has seen your content, you can put ads in front of them. These ads could drive to a variety of pages. It could be to a webinar, a self-liquidating offer, a training series, an events page, lead magnets—whatever it is, the purpose is to gain a commitment from your prospect in the form of a purchase or their information. You should invest about 25 percent of your budget into this step.

RETARGETING: STAYING IN FRONT OF YOUR AUDIENCE

The goal of the Retargeting step is to:

- Stay top of mind inside your prospect's world
- Reach the majority of the leads who do not convert immediately

Many customers do not buy right away—they may need time to think, to research, to get to know your brand better. Sometimes your core marketing message won't speak to what they want.

The first objective of Retargeting is to stay top of mind. When your audience sees you multiple times, they begin to like you naturally. By simply staying top of mind, you'll generate more sales. The second objective is to reach the majority of the leads who do not convert immediately. These leads may have objections, doubts, or questions that are unanswered. With retargeting ads, you'll target these objections and loose ends to give those sitting on the fence a final push.

If you have a premium offer, then your customers will have many different reasons for buying. There are many reasons people join our program. They join because they want to learn a new skill, better their relationships, join a positive and supportive community, challenge themselves, grow their business, or a dozen other reasons. If our marketing spoke to only one of these reasons for buying, we'd be half as big as we are today. In our retargeting strategy, we rotate our ads and make sure we scratch every itch our audience has. This allows us to capture a majority of sales that would have otherwise disappeared. Allocate about 25 percent of your budget if you decide to implement this strategy.

WHERE DO YOU GO FROM HERE?

There's not enough room in this book to show you in detail everything we do. If you want to learn more about how I build and scale my social capital, the best way is to follow me—you can do so at danlok.com/social.

I've also prepared additional training for those who want to learn more in depth about social capital and scaling their business. You can find this at unlockitbook.com/resources.

Conclusion

Congratulations! First, I want to acknowledge you for finishing the book. Most people leave books unfinished, but you're different. I have truly given you the keys to unlock your success, wealth, and significance. I've shared with you how I think, the lessons I've learned in life, and my business views.

Now that you have the keys, you have the Unlock It mind-set as well. Whenever you're stuck, whenever you hit an obstacle, whenever you're facing a problem, you know there's a solution, and that you need to find the right key to unlock it.

You have the key to your life—the master key is you. You are the master key to unlocking everything you want in life. Whether it's more freedom, more success, more money, more significance, more relationships, more health, more impact, or more anything, you are in control.

Now, you have a choice. You can either forget everything I've just shared with you or you can apply the lessons and take action. Maybe you want to unlock your productivity, develop your High-Income Skill, or structure your business differently so it can scale faster. Whatever your goal is, I hope this is the beginning of our relationship and that we can take this beyond just a book. We can stay connected on social media, or you can join one of our virtual trainings, or you could even attend one of our events. Whatever it is, let me know how I could best serve you, and I look forward to furthering our relationship.

Until then, keep learning, keep implementing, and keep taking action.

Index